The Dance of Parenting

Finding Your Inner Choreographer

Natasha Solovieff

BALBOA.
PRESS
A DIVISION OF HAY HOUSE

Balboa Press books may be ordered through booksellers or by contacting:

Balboa Press
A Division of Hay House
1663 Liberty Drive
Bloomington, IN 47403
www.balboapress.com
1 (877) 407-4847

Because of the dynamic nature of the Internet, any web addresses or links contained in this book may have changed since publication and may no longer be valid. The views expressed in this work are solely those of the author and do not necessarily reflect the views of the publisher, and the publisher hereby disclaims any responsibility for them.

The author of this book does not dispense medical advice or prescribe the use of any technique as a form of treatment for physical, emotional, or medical problems without the advice of a physician, either directly or indirectly. The intent of the author is only to offer information of a general nature to help you in your quest for emotional and spiritual well-being. In the event you use any of the information in this book for yourself, which is your constitutional right, the author and the publisher assume no responsibility for your actions.

Any people depicted in stock imagery provided by Thinkstock are models, and such images are being used for illustrative purposes only. Certain stock imagery © Thinkstock.

Print information available on the last page.

ISBN: 978-1-5043-7435-4 (sc)
ISBN: 978-1-5043-7436-1 (e)

Library of Congress Control Number: 2017901991

Balboa Press rev. date: 04/24/2017

CONTENTS

ACKNOWLEDGEMENTS

Writing a book is never a solo journey. From the beginning my sister Tanya cheered on the idea of me writing this book. My sister Nadya jumped in with some ideas for organizing my writing process which were enormously helpful. The curiosity of my friends as I went through this helped me formulate thoughts.

Particularly important has been my mastermind group led by Lauren L'Amour. She and they cheered, gently probed and prodded which helped me move through the terror fences I met. They also kept me at the keyboard even if sometimes for just fifteen minutes a day. I think they are with me for life!

Then there were those spontaneous, passionate comments from my daughter. Inevitably they'd lead to conversations that inspired me. Inspiring me is something she's been doing since she was born.

Of course a book doesn't even make it to a publisher without a good edit or two or three. For that I thank Kathe Connair, editor, lover of books and a Mom. She helped me organize the book, using her fine toothed comb to find what made sense and to correct all the run-on sentences! Additionally, the very fine tooth comb of Daniel Born, editor, professor and father, found my inconsistent grammar.

I also want to thank the parents everywhere who have dared to share their vulnerability with me. To protect confidentiality, all names are fictional and the stories are representative rather than literal. I've found that parenting stories are universal, and I share these with the utmost respect.

INTRODUCTION

When I started this book, my daughter was 22 years old. Our household had been loaded with kids (her friends) throughout those years. In addition to parenting a lively household, I have worked with more parents over the years than I can count. Because of this personal and professional journey, I find that as I "close out" parenting, I've got a lot to say! I can reflect now from a different vantage point than I did during active parenting. I feel good about what has happened, mostly; but I acknowledge that there were some phases when I could have gotten more support for myself and thereby been less exhausted, less worn down about my sense of success as a parent. I am hoping to spare you that exhaustion and loss of self-esteem! Actually, not to spare you, because some parenting pitfalls seem to be a part of the parenting path. But I do hope to give you a way through these parenting pitfalls that gently enhances and enlivens your life.

As you read this book, you may be pregnant and wondering, how do I do this parenting thing? You may be considering adoption or are just bringing your adopted child home. You may have a toddler who is full of himself or herself, whose demands set all kinds of limits on *you* when you thought you were supposed to be the one setting the limits. You might have a tween and things are starting to get a bit topsy turvy and you wonder, how do I get ahead of this and prepare for the teen years? You may be in the roller-coaster ride known as the teen years and wondering, what's happened to my world? You may be in love with your child. Or you may be wondering where that love went.

No matter what your starting point is, through engaging with this book you will find ways to create peace in the chaos of current-day family life and to find harmonious, customized ways to deal with whatever is challenging you. Life is a customized experience, after all!

You are about to explore and strengthen the use of your core parenting capacities. These are the skills you will draw on during all phases of your child's development, whether you have simple or complex challenges. You can start to use these skills no matter how much you know about childhood development and what it takes to be a parent. Using them will increase your confidence, strengthen your intuition, intention, and your parenting intelligence. All of this is needed in today's fast-paced, information-laden world.

What's a capacity? The definitions provided by the Oxford Dictionary include: the ability to receive, hold, or absorb; the ability to do something (as in the capacity for self-expression); the ability to learn.

To me, capacity has to do with the being, not so much the doing, of parenting. Or said another way, strengthening these capacities changes the "doing" of being a parent.

This book does not provide the typical "to-do" list for parents (read to your child daily, use feeling words for your and their behaviors, set a homework routine, choose your battles with consequences you can stick with). Rather it focuses more on common pitfalls of parenting and ways through them that will strengthen your powers. That strength will come from your ability to be calm, hear between the words, look outside the box of input from others and your own fears, use the power of your thoughts and feelings to maintain harmony in your home, and empower yourself in your relationships with loved ones and others engaged with your children; your use of intuition, intention, and parenting intelligence.

I still pay attention to my parenting by honing my core parenting capacities. I learned a lot from all these parenting years. Additionally, I have been working as a clinical and public health nurse for over twenty years, working with families. I've been looking into the faces of babies, parents, and grandparents. I have felt their joys, hopes, disappointments, traumas, grief, fears, concerns, laughter, and love. I have heard their thoughts, their expectations, their discipline struggles. I have seen their actions and the effects of those actions. I have interacted with the many kinds of professionals who weave in and out of family life. Because of all of this, I have a great appreciation for the range of inner experience within parenting, as well as the range of relationship experience between parents and their children.

This book is an answer to my wonderings about what makes some parents strong and happy with their lot and others distressed and tense. I've seen parents who have children with behavioral or health challenges be strong and happy. I've seen parents who seemingly have it all who are tense. I have concluded that developing certain capacities of love – the skills and practices of love, if you will – is the key to being in the laughter, affection, connectedness, calm, and life-expanding growth that comes from parenting. I have seen that these capacities are central to moving on when disappointments and tough times are real. I have seen that developing these capacities allows some parents to thrive and even have fun through all of the ups and downs.

While no book can sum up everything about parenting, I am offering activities here that will give you a strong parenting core. It's not a one-time use book. You can return as often as needed.

I want to acknowledge, up front, that there are indeed parenting challenges for which it might not matter, in terms of outcome, how much you develop these capacities. You can't control others or the impact of life's events. You can't control all the variables that come up in your kid's life. The outcome you would dearly love for them might not be what you get. Addiction is real, mental health variations are real, temperament management challenges are real, abuse is real, effects of community violence are real. However, I can guarantee that development of these capacities will always matter in terms of your *own* behavior and how you feel about your parenting success within the life variables you meet.

Whether your challenges consist of weighty matters like addiction and abuse or the more everyday challenges that come up with your children, in doing the practices laid out in the second section of the book, the workbook section, you will be

✓ less stressed,

- ✓ more fully informed,
- ✓ less frustrated and lost
- ✓ empowered to grow your relationship with your child in a loving way
- ✓ liberated from some of the things that keep you from enjoying your child
- ✓ empowered to grow your own life
- ✓ laughing more
- ✓ trusting your intuition
- ✓ motivated by your parenting intentions
- ✓ feeling pretty darn intelligent

In the first section of this book, I take a look at some challenging feelings about the experience of parenting that I've seen arise among parents across all economic groups and ethnicities. I'll tell you a bit about how some parents have used what I call the L.O.V.E. capacities to help them surmount those challenges. And in Chapter 3, I'll introduce the young mom whose experiences helped me develop the idea for the dance of parenting and what it feels like.

In the second section, you will be prompted to **pick a challenge in your parenting experience that you will track** as you read. That way you can use the various levels of practices/activities to strengthen your core parenting capacities and to positively alter the stress you're experiencing. This exercise will work whether you pick something that is *really* challenging you with your kids or if you begin with a *lesser* challenge – one that you know will be easier to work through.

The core capacities you are about to engage in are Listening, OMing, Voicing and Visualizing, and Exploring. Yep, it spells the word LOVE. I didn't plan it that way ... really! That emerged from a lengthy list of what I thought it took to be positively, consciously engaged in parenting. As I whittled away at it, much to my delight, I saw the word LOVE.

In the second section, each capacity is broken down into a description of what it means, what happens if you don't develop it, what happens when you do develop it, and three to four levels of practices for strengthening it. You'll even get some of the science behind it all. Plus, all those bennies listed above will be yours if you keep returning to these practices over the next three to six months.

Enjoy LOVEing up your parenting!

SECTION 1

WHEN THE DANCE
IS OUT OF STEP

RECOGNIZING WE'RE OUT OF STEP

In this section of *The Dance of Parenting*, you will read about commonly held ideas and feelings that become pitfalls in parenting. Pitfalls occur when a mom, dad, or someone in a parenting role has normal vulnerabilities in which they get stuck. Vulnerabilities are things that are causing significant uncertainty and doubt. When we get stuck in them, it can undermine our enjoyment of parenting not to mention ripple over into our relationship with ourselves and our children. We are not in our harmonious dance of parenting; the harmonious dance is like that waltz that just flows even when we misstep or improvise movement.

The stories in this section are from my professional experience, things parents have told me as I just wander around, and from my personal experience. Except for my own stories, all names are fictionalized.

1

By reading about these very normal vulnerabilities, missteps, and reflecting on their presence in our parenting, we begin to achieve progress toward our harmonious dance. And that is the trick: noticing when we are out of step and finding our way back into step (section two).

The way back into step is through strengthening your innate L.O.V.E. capacities through purposeful practice. Those practices are are identified in parentheses throughout the stories discussed in Section One. In Section Two, a number of those purposeful practices are developed in more specific detail. I recommend reading the stories in Section One first.

The L.O.V.E. capacities are Listening, OMing, Visualizing, Voicing, and Exploring. You will get an idea of what those mean in the next couple of chapters. Frankly, their meaning keeps deepening as you use them.

CHAPTER 1

THE DANCE

DANCING REQUIRES YOUR CORE!

Parenting is a bit like a dance. As mothers and fathers, we move closer to our children at times and farther from them at other times. Sometimes we move gracefully in our role, and other times we are just out of step with our children. And, like dancing, there are times when it's fun, oh yes! We know that sometimes the dance can be soft and gentle or zippy and exhilarating. Other times you might feel stuck, like you have two right feet (think toddlers and teens!). And you might need to improvise on the spot! As is true for dancers, so is it true for parents: working from our core keeps us and our partners healthy, uninjured. In parenting, though, the core we're talking about is a state of mind, not physical. However, like every dancer, every parent must develop their core and build skills through practice.

The *Dance of Parenting* is about how we utilize and strengthen our core capacities that are in fact innate and essential to parenting. It's about associated exercises to practice, in order to ease our parenting experience, to keep the dance with our children flowing. Practice inspires confidence and lets us keep more fun, more enjoyment, and more of our heart's desire in the dance. It also makes it easier to minimize the stress, anxiety, worry, conflict, and disconnectedness we might feel with our children. And it helps us grow stronger and more liberated even as our children grow more solidly into their independent dance with life.

Notice you don't need to *acquire* anything, you just need to *develop* what you already have. It's just a matter of becoming more aware of and practicing some things that strengthen your already present capacities to Listen, OM, Visualize and Voice, and Explore - your capacity to L.O.V.E. These capacities are like endless wells of energy waiting to be used.

Using these energy wells to empower your parenting dance is like any creative act: It takes having an idea of the result you want, dealing with uncertainty of how you will achieve that end (although you have some ideas), being open to the moment and to learning new things (including about yourself), meeting hard times, loving the easy times. And through it all your core self comes through more and more. Many times the creative journey is an adventure full of things you weren't expecting with upsides and downsides. The dance of parenting is a creative adventure!

And it's ongoing. We are continuously creating our family life through our parenting dance. Is that dance fluid, flowing, jerky, aggressive, slow, fast? It is all of these things, different moods showing up at different times (like a really good dance).

In the following chapters, we'll first examine some of the challenges that get in the way of our heart's desire for the ultimate dance - the easy exchange described in Chapter 3. Secondly, in chapters 10-14, you'll use your L.O.V.E. capacities to resolve parenting challenges and get back in the groove more quickly than you might think.

The checklist that you see next gives a hint of what it's like to have those capacities fully developed, but honestly, when you are into full-blown use of them, you will find yourself adding things to the checklist. Or, you might say, it just is what it is and these parts of me have worked wonders!

MY CAPACITY USE BEFORE AND AFTER

The first two columns are for now and the other two are for a later date of your choosing.

I do this:	Yes	No	Yes	No
I just listen to my child, without saying anything, at least once a day.				
I summarize to my child what I am "hearing" him or her say.				
When I am not getting responses from my child, I come up with different ways.				
I teach my child to tell me if they want me to just listen or to give advice.				
I point out my child's strengths.				
I breathe as a way to pause when things are tense.				
I practice closing my eyes so I can just feel my child in my mind's eye.				
I become aware of my inner conversation about my child.				
I use intentional visualization throughout my parenting.				
I talk to trusted others I can talk to about my child.				
I examine my feelings, as well as my thoughts, about potential solutions.				
I am usually aware of how my fears are "inspiring" my reactions.				

I turn my fears into the five affirmations.				
I am willing to let my child experience natural consequences.				
I explore safety issues by asking my child "what would you do if" questions.				
I question in mind when looking at new information.				
I breathe as a way to pause when things are tense				
I become aware my inner conversations about my child				
I become aware of the 'mind videos' that play in my mind about my child				
My children and I talk regularly about their days easy and difficult things				
I take care of myself, expressing my needs without demeaning my children				
I have practices in place that support me in being loving				

CHAPTER 2

THE L.O.V.E. CAPACITIES

You already have these capacities, being the incredible human being that you are! Here is a brief description of each (there's much more on each later in the book). To make it up close and personal, each capacity is described in terms of what we tend to say and do when using it.

Chapter 2-1

Your Capacity	What You Say	What You Do
Listening	Not much! But when you do it's reflective: "Let me see if I am getting this straight. You are telling me ..."	Zip your lips. Use all your senses.

O*Ming*	I need to get off the world for a bit. I need to step away from this. I need to go deeper.	Stop what you are doing. Get quiet inside (there are a multitude of ways). Stay in that quiet space for a bit. Re-emerge refreshed.
V*isualizing*	What am I imagining? What movies are playing in my head? What do I really want here? Of what I can control, how do I see this playing out?	Close your eyes. Notice what you are imagining. Re-imagine your part according to what you want.
V*oicing*	Am I saying this in a way that can be heard? What am I not saying and why?	Get feedback. Pay attention to your motivation.

As you read through that, you probably noticed that you already do some of these things. That's what I mean! You do indeed have these wells of energy. Funny thing is, as we move through parenting and meet different challenges, we forget to use them.

There seem to be many reasons for that:

1. **It isn't a part of our culture** to talk about these things (more on that in Chapter 4: How Big Is the Stage).
2. **We're uncomfortable** closing our eyes and hearing/seeing what is going on in our mind.
3. **We expect to just "be the parent,"** wielding authority, and are thrown when we feel vulnerable or unsure about how to handle something. We think we should be teachers, but we are learning, too.
4. **We believe feeling love is enough.** Philosophers can argue the point. But for our purposes, let's say there's more to parenting than that bond. We need to know how to get our parenting self into a place of love when we are angry, worried, scared out of our minds, feeling undervalued, and wondering if we're doing it right. Love has process to it! We need to learn how to access these capacities, our energy wells, and how to use the good stuff once we've gotten hold of it.
5. **We freeze when we're scared out of our minds** about something. Could it be that our child's mental health, tech habits, grades in school, progression through milestones, friendships ... are just filling us with so many reactions that we don't know where to begin?
6. **Parenting is about "other."** Learning to apply things like visualization, which typically is self-focused, to parenting can be confusing.
7. **Our expectations of parenting** could keep us from problem solving. If we idealize its loving nature, we might deny when there is tension or discord. Or if we expect there to be discord, we might just toss it off as normal. As one mom said: "Worry comes with loving your kids, doesn't it?"
8. **Our families think we're crazy.** A little too woo-woo for them. This is especially hard if it's our parenting partner who doesn't want to discuss how to stay in the parenting love zone.

CHAPTER 3

DANCING IN THE LOVE ZONE

DANCE IMPROV!

The dance of parenting, when flowing, is like a dance improvisation, as this mother showed me. She was a 16-year-old mother, yet as I watched her interact with her son during our meeting, I saw a beautiful dance unfold in front of me. Such a give and take it was!

He sat by the computer, pretending he was doing something on it. Occasionally she would look at him and he back at her. Both would grin.

He arrived at our table with the computer mouse in his hand. She nodded and asked him to put it back. Of course, being only 20 months old, he had to take the long route to the desk. That meant crawling over a chair, under a coffee table, and circling round to look out the window. Mom kept up her glances and smiles and gentle reminders until he did indeed drop the mouse off at the right computer. "Thank you," she said.

We continued talking throughout all of this. He then got a little vigorous with the window blinds, so she went over, looked outside with him, and told him not to bang on the blinds like that because they would break. When he stopped, she relocated him to the kitchen, giving him a hug en route. This dance had some different steps, but they did it in sync.

Once in the kitchen, he played for quite a while with the plastic containers and pots. Mom occasionally shifted in her chair to say something to him and he waltzed between her and the kitchen. Just checking in.

As I was leaving, I told her that she and her son had a wonderful rapport and that I was struck by how finely in tune they were with each other. She was not at all annoyed by his cues that he needed her, requiring her presence to set limits or wandering along the way as he completed a requested task (all age appropriate). Their movements were very busy, yet had a sense of peace and ease to them.

As they came and went from each other, giving and taking, leading and following, I saw a beautiful dance; they were in the love zone! Their "dance" flowed, even as they turned away from each other to engage in something else for a bit before returning to each other. It was a soft dance, this love.

We all come and go from this kind of parenting dance during our child-raising years. For most of us, the dance begins with a lullaby. We are so in love with our baby that we float through their ups and downs with the greatest of ease (unless they are colicky or by temperament a bit fussier). This is the love zone dance that we dream of and gravitate toward; it is pleasantly exhausting, fulfilling, joyful and fun. We relish those moments of being so in sync.

As with most dances, though, things change. A different day we are more tired; our child is strutting their toddler oats or their teen "I can do this alone." Parenting is very real, with good, smooth-steppin' days and bad, stumbling days.

Yet, if we are aware of where we are at in the dance, and what is influencing it, we might more readily get back in sync when we're out of step. We also feel more acknowledged in our parenting role, as well as more accepting of our child's natural state at that particular time in life.

When I asked this mom how she learned to parent this way, she said, "I know I want to listen to him, and I just want to love him and have fun." She developed her Listen capacity because it was something she felt was lacking in her parents. I pointed out to her that she also read and talked about parenting (using her Explore capacity). I asked her what she does when she gets upset. She said, "I take a deep breath (her OM capacity), and then I say something to him (her Voice capacity)." She came to her parenting dance very naturally.

Kudos to her! She knew from her reading that toddlers need to stay close and yet explore, to receive help and yet be independent. She also knew her son needed limits because she had observed other parents and their children. And she had developed a vision (her Vision capacity) of a loving relationship. So she just took deep breaths rather than get angry about something that was natural for her son. It was beautiful to behold.

She had been surprised and chagrined when she got pregnant. But when she accepted it, she got on with the business of becoming a parent. She started growing her L.O.V.E. capacities without even being conscious of it. And yet, there was a point when she realized she wanted more support with parenting. It's like that for a lot of us.

We start our pregnancy with our L.O.V.E. capacities fully dancing. "I'm pregnant!" we announce. Or, if we are adopting, "They have a baby/child for us to meet!" And there begins the most dramatic experience of our lives: parenting.

We start actively parenting from the very first efforts to make room in our lives for a child, from facing our fears about labor and delivery or the uncertainties of adoption, to experiencing the heart-opening joy of meeting him or her.

This is true even if we aren't too excited about becoming a parent at first; the timing might not be quite what we wanted, or we're worried about postpartem depression, or there is conflict with our partner in parenting. Our L.O.V.E. capacities may be more challenged, but they are within us and we can access them.

I remember it well, that moment the stick turned pink and, although I didn't think about them as L.O.V.E. capacities then, they kicked in with full force. We had tried to get pregnant several months the previous year and stopped because I didn't like the emotional up and down of anticipation and disappointment. So this pink stick was particularly wonderful. And I flushed with the thrill when my husband said, "I knew it, there's just been something different about you."

We had talked quite a lot about parenting, so we had a pretty well-developed idea (Vision) of how we wanted to do it, the environment we wanted to create.

And then, of course, the fears kicked in (part of Vision, too). Being a nurse who had worked in a neonatal intensive care unit (NICU), I was especially concerned about baby development because I was past 36 years old (although, honestly, in my 12 years in a NICU, young women accounted for most of the premature babies, so to this day I am puzzled by the statistics linking older mothers to higher incidences of premature birth and defects).

We also had some of the standard concerns about money and work schedules. I was in management and had some new projects rolling out, so I worried about how my workplace would deal with the need for leadership.

No matter what our germinating experience is, everything changes the moment we know we are pregnant: how we see the world, think of ourselves, feel toward our mates, view our life purpose, and experience our bodies.

As our baby develops within us, we move in and out of excitement, fear, overwhelmedness, confidence, changes in our relationship with our partners. The baby picks up on how we are responding to our moods and activities, changing its own activity levels depending on what we are feeling and doing.

And we, in turn, start to notice how the baby is responding. Yes! The parenting dance has begun. So it is time to intentionally get in sync with our L.O.V.E. capacities: Listening, OM Moments, Visualizing and Voicing, and Exploring. We already have every single one of these capacities and are in fact using them all the time. Yet, as parents, we have to learn more about them to grow them, to expand and enlarge our use of them, to become more sensitive to them. If we don't, we can still parent. We will just find ourselves depleted rather than energized, overwhelmed rather than enjoying the process, worrying rather than trusting, responding more often with irritation rather than with love. And our children will suffer from that as well as us.

For instance, some people are consumed by worry, starting during pregnancy. Will I be a good parent? Will there be enough money? Will my partner still think I'm attractive? Will the guys at work think me less intelligent? Will my shape return? Will life ever be normal again? What if there are birth defects?

Worry, however, can take the joy out of anything, pregnancy and parenting included. It fatigues us. It doesn't help solve anything. It takes us out of the Love Zone dance. It takes us further out of the ring of L.O.V.E. around our parenting. It's a paradox because we often feel that we worry because we love! If that is you right now, I encourage you to do some of the Visioning and OM moments practices in the second section of the book. Because, indeed the dance we want going on from pregnancy forward, the dance we want to know well within ourselves, is the Love Zone dance.

I think about Sally, a pregnant woman in her 30s. She was very ambivalent about being pregnant again. Her work life was just firming up, she'd just gotten back into shape after her first pregnancy, she and her husband had found a rhythm around parenting together. She loved her little guy. She was even enjoying sleeping more because teething was over! She knew she was reacting very differently to this pregnancy than the first one. "Why did I switch birth control," she admonished herself.

Because she wanted to embrace the pregnancy, she took a deep breath and committed to listening to herself and letting the layers of what she heard unfold. After a while, she started to accept her feelings and started being able to use her OM moments to "listen" to the baby within her. Then she started to see how the vision she and her husband had for future children could be a now thing, instead of worrying about the future. By letting all the different feelings come up, giving voice to them, she let them sift and sort. She took the first steps in her Love Zone dance with this baby. She got it; she understood that when you use your L.O.V.E. capacities, your dance with your child is easier, more fun, and more fulfilling.

When having a lot of feelings all at once, like Sally did, it's best to just take the time to pay attention to each of them instead of trying to identify the dominant feeling. By paying attention to each of them, your whole feeling world starts to shift around and the dominant feeling will naturally rise to the top. A therapist told me this once and it's been a stress saver for me as I frequently experience multiple feelings at the same time. When Sally tried this, she was able to get to a point where she didn't judge herself for her sometimes contradictory feelings. And much to her surprise, her vision of becoming a mother changed. She got excited about it and found solutions to the things that concerned her the most.

14

That's part of what expanding our parenting L.O.V.E. capacities does: it opens us up to new feelings and leads to solutions that we couldn't have imagined before. Sally was able to move around in the L.O.V.E. capacities. As a result, she found her parenting L.O.V.E. dance and enlarged her ability to love herself.

That's what the young Mom I mentioned at the beginning of this chapter did with her son quite naturally. There was so much self-acceptance and acceptance of her son, so much mutual attunement, so much flow. What a great dance! The exercises in the latter part of this book will help you get to a similar place with your worries and challenges.

Central to this dance is that attunement between parent and child. I was with one mom whose car had stalled. Her son ran around on the nearby grass while others focused on the car. She became worried that he might run into the busy street and asked him to come closer. He didn't want to. She took him by the hand. He screamed at the top of his lungs. I looked up and there she stood, still, quietly holding his hand while he screamed. Eventually, he stopped. They hugged and he stayed at her side. I was struck by the peace, the acceptance, the "this is okay, it just is what it is" feeling in her as she gently held his hand, looking straight ahead. I thought to myself, a mom in the Love Zone. How beautiful!

Love, even when it comes naturally, is not something that grows without attention, without nurturing. Just like a dance, it takes practice. Author Ursula K. Le Guin says, "Love doesn't just sit there, like a stone, it has to be made, like bread; remade all the time, made new."[1]

The *Dance of Parenting* is about nurturing ourselves with practices that grow our L.O.V.E. capacities. We grow and change because we are engaged in parenting. We are challenged by the world our children are growing up in, by how they are different from us, by our own need to evolve. There is so much that can pull us out of step during our dance in the parenting love zone. If we want to nurture our developing, ever changing children, we must become aware of our L.O.V.E. practices.

The next few chapters focus on some of the challenges we commonly experience that get us out of sync. In turn, those chapters are followed by steps that can return us to more graceful motion.

CHAPTER 4

WHAT STAGE ARE WE ON?

Why do we parent the way we do? Why do we do maternity leave the way we do? Why do we believe in peer-based play dates (instead of multi-aged play dates)? Why do we start our kids in competitive sports at age five? Why do we believe mothers should stay home rather than work? Why do we feel shy about breastfeeding?

The answer is culture. Culture refers to a generally accepted way of social and artistic expression. There are behavior patterns, beliefs, institutions, arts, and products and services thought to be characteristic of a nation, a community, a family. For instance, it is culturally accepted that Swedish mothers won't work for a year after having a baby, and that fathers get ample time off, too. In the United States, it's back to work after one or two weeks for dads and four to six weeks for moms. Another example is that in many countries, kids of all ages play with each other. Here, we find ourselves setting up play dates among for children of the same age.

Our expectations of ourselves and our children are often set by our culture. We picked up these expectations just by moving through life, many times without even knowing we are doing this. That's neither good nor bad, but expectations can be a source of tension or judgment as well as guidance, so it's worth it to become aware of cultural influences.

First, where do we get those expectations from? It is said that we parent based on how we were parented. At least, that is our starting point.

Do you recall when you were pregnant, or planning to bring home your adopted child, thinking about what you would do the same as your parents, or differently? "I'll never do/say that," we say to ourselves. Or, "I loved that about my family" we say.

So our own experience of being a child sets us up in the culture of parenting acceptable to those around us.

As we grow and learn, some of those ideas shift. That has been going on since the beginning of family life.

Consider this: In ancient Rome (753 B.C. - 476 A.D.), a father held absolute power over his children; he could discipline them as he wished, sell them into slavery, even kill them. Using "the rod" to punish one's child was expected. The Romans considered childhood over at around 13 years of age, at which point parents wanted their girls married off and their boys to be schooled in some adult pursuit. These behaviors and beliefs were the norm.

Back then, girls were only valued in terms of marriage and reproduction. When concerns were raised that bodily punishment might make children hardened, like slaves, the term "children" referred only to boys, not girls. [2]

Today, all of this would be considered abusive.

Even by Renaissance times (the 1300s - 1600s), attitudes had not changed much. You can see some of the roots of our current parenting culture forming in the late 1800s. In the Victorian period, children were "meant to be seen, not heard." In *The Book of Household Management* (1861), author Isabella Beeton described fathers as generally distant and reserved.[3] They were the disciplinarians, though, and were respectfully addressed by their children as "Mr." or "Sir." Mothers were "Ma'm" and they were at the fore of parenting, where character building was the main focus. It was the mom's job, along with teachers (largely female), to impart a strict routine of schoolroom studies and lessons in morality. Thus, even in households with a nanny, mom was accountable for the children's behavior. (This continues to be true. When things go wrong, mom is still the first to be blamed.) [4]

But eventually parents began to be invested in their children's emotional and psychological well-being. In the early 1900s, concerns about personality development and gender identity (boys will be boys, etc.) permeated parenting. The field of child psychology came into being and had a huge influence on parenting culture. Mothers still have the primary responsibility for our children's development, fulfilling emotional and psychological needs, but fathers are getting more involved, especially as more than one million now stay at home with their kids.

Along with the expanding field of child development, we are seeing an explosion in scientific and spiritual findings. We live in an era alive with information about what makes a human being tick! There is a growing amount of research on what parental interactions aid or hinder a child's development. Technology has allowed us to see into the brain as well as to study intricate biochemical interactions and genetic details. These discoveries influence what we focus on as parents. For example, we now know that Vitamin B supplements are desirable during the toddler and teen years when there is intense brain development and a risk of learning disabilities. The information (and misinformation) we have access to is amazing. It has, however, added to the intensity of parenting, increasing the sense of urgency about how to best be a parent.

With so much technology added to an already hectic pace of life, it is essential that parents find a way to step back from all this urgency about their kids - the urgency to do it right, to have this and be that.

Staying in the L.O.V.E. Zone and getting to the right answers is actually simple. It may not feel easy at first, but it becomes easier after using the practices in the second part of the book. So congratulations for engaging in this! The alternative is extreme fatigue, disconnection with your children as they age, feeling powerless, a decline in your health, and more stress instead of more fun.

Of course, when we talk about culture, it is in broad generalities. We don't all beat to the same drum (cultural understandings), nor have parents throughout history. But culture does influence our parenting, our families, and technology is influencing our culture a lot now. One of its effects on parents is confusion: There is so much information available, decision-making can be challenging. For instance, have you ever had one of the following experiences?

Your child:

- isn't doing well in all his classes. Since sixth grade, your child's teachers have been talking about how competitive college is but there are different points of view about the importance of college.
- is a brat when you say "no" to something she wants, she neeeeeds. Your budget is limited, but there's so much pressure to "keep up with the Joneses" in the kid world and you don't want her to feel left out.
- is not interested in sports and wants to play video games all the time. When you tell him to find something else to do, all holy hell breaks loose. You wonder, Is this an addiction? All the experts say something different.
- is not eating healthful foods and says he's just eating what everyone eats. Whenever you talk with him about it, you wind up fighting.
- wants a really big birthday party but you don't have the energy, or see the need for it. And frankly, you would rather spend the money on something else.

The culture you live in can shape your answers to all of these. For instance, is college valued? The national culture might support the idea of college, but where you live, people might place more value on getting a job that contributes to family needs. Because these broad differences in culture can exist, it's important to know which influences us as we respond to parenting challenges.

Big birthday parties may be a must in your social circle. That's culture talking.

And culture changes! Hence, so-called "generation gaps." Over my life span, I have seen a few things that make parenting different now than in previous generations. It used to be that you got a job and stuck with that company for the duration of your career. That is no longer true. It is commonly said that people will change the focus of their work seven times during their lives. And changing jobs is high on the list of big stressors. And big stressors can affect our parenting.

Cultural changes show up when we look at kids' play time. It used to be that kids played outside a lot, roaming for hours, unsupervised. That is no longer true, due to stranger danger concerns. This is a logistical stress and source of worry for parents now.

It used to be that you went to the grocery store and bought food that you trusted was healthy. Now you practically need a degree in nutrition to run a healthy household.

It used to be that you went to the family doctor for just about everything. Now there is so much conflicting medical advice that it takes a lot more time to find trusted resources.

Because parenting dilemmas affected by culture go on and on, it is essential that parents find their way to step back from the pace and urgency of information. Developing all of your L.O.V.E. capacities is so valuable to dealing with today's parenting environment.

Our kids are bombarded with a lot. *You,* parents, are bombarded with a lot. What's important is yes, that you get answers, but first, that you find your way to stay in the L.O.V.E. Zone while pursuing answers. Because life is definitely a customized experience now. The answer that's right for one child might not be right for the other one. The answer that's right for one family isn't necessarily right for another.

Staying in the L.O.V.E. Zone while navigating all of this is what it's all about. We all want to thrive in our parenting. We want to have energy, be connected to our children as they age, feel empowered, and have more fun than stress. And we want to move our own lives forward at the same time!

The following are some questions to help you determine what aspect of culture might be affecting your parenting. It could be an aspect of our national culture, but it could be based in your local community or your family. For instance, Americans are very shy (some might say adversarial) about breastfeeding. Now. But nursing in public seemed to be a non-issue in colonial America[5].

Or, if your family conversations involve a lot of sass, that may cause problems in school where national norms call for more respectful discussion. Knowing which culture is influencing your parenting is important.

Culture gives us a very large stage on which we do our dance of parenting. It's a great place to start questioning why you are dancing this way or that. Here are some general questions to get the ball rolling.[6] You can use these when contemplating the culture of your family life, community life, spiritual community, your child's school/class, or your country.

1. What are the norms around parenting; what really stands out as being important or unimportant?
   a. You can get at this by knowing what your parents did that you want to carry on AND what they did that you don't want to carry on.
2. How are gender roles perceived?
3. Which is more encouraged, action or contemplation?
4. What are the criteria for success?
5. What is considered fun? How would you describe it: aggressive, collaborative, competitive, physical, mental, creative?
6. Are rules followed by the book or meant to be questioned?
7. What contributions are important/valued/admired?

The issue of cultural influences is important to understand, because whether you are aligned with or differ from your surrounding culture affects your stress level, your sense of success, and your plan for unfolding what is important to you and your immediate family. Cultural beliefs can pull people together, but they can also create a great divide between parents and between generations. The above questions can be used to open a dialogue when there is conflict between you and your parenting partners, including your child's grandparents!

Keep these questions in mind as you move through the next five chapters on common issues that affect your dance of parenting. How you handle these issues may be influenced by big bits of culture.

CHAPTER 5

NO TIME FOR ME

Everywhere I go I hear mothers say, "My life doesn't belong to me." There is a bit of reality to that, isn't there? A mom who likes quiet mornings doesn't exactly get that when her child comes in, pokes her in the eye, and says, "Wake up, Mom." Vacation bliss can go out the window when a teen can't make the effort to even smile. A date night out gets disrupted when the babysitter calls to say a child is vomiting.

We have lots of proof that our time is not our own. Over the years, I wondered how to reconcile this with all the messages about balance and self-care. For many mothers, self-care is just one more thing to do; it takes a certain amount of energy to pay attention to one's self!

Over the centuries, moms have always been in the position of giving a lot, putting aside many of their desires. It is a cultural imperative for many; witness the judgments that go on between SAHM (stay-at-home moms) and WFTM (work-full-time moms) and even WAHM (work-at-home moms). We are so confused about what is okay! What can we do to find our own individual and household peace with this issue?

There is no biological imperative for mothers to stay at home — or go to work or work at home. Because of the oxytocin in a mother's system, though, there is a biological imperative to nurture and care for her child. Often that nurturing takes us outside of our own natural rhythms, though. For Lisa, who is an introvert, "It's exhausting keeping up with" her daughter, who is an extrovert. For Laura, who goes with the flow and likes the adventure of unplanned days, it's "humorous on good days and disastrous on bad days" because her high school-age daughter likes to have things all planned out.

So how do we nurture and care for these very absorbing beings, our children, and take care of ourselves, too? Without feeling guilty about it? And is this only a mother's dilemma?

Fathers are, thankfully, becoming more involved in their children's lives than ever before. According to the National Stay at Home Dad Network, 1.4 million were intentionally staying at home to care for their children in 2009. There are more now, I am sure. A Boston College study from 2012 says that 70 percent of these fathers are staying at home with their kids by choice, not because they have lost a job or didn't have one to begin with.[7]

So, do SAHDs feel they have no time for themselves? Not from what I have read. The conflicts and dismays are experienced differently by this group of culture warriors who dare to go against our expectations.

Author and stay-at-home-dad Brian Gresko says men have it easier. "The term 'stay-at-home dad' carries less freight than stay-at-home mom," he writes. "There's no 'daddy wars,' for example, the way moms battle it out, at least rhetorically, online, about whether being a working mom is somehow a disservice to your children. As a dad, you still get points for just showing up, which is a remnant of sexism. That's changing, slowly. Too slowly, I think."[8]

Leslie Morgan Steiner points out how another author, caregiver, and household manager, Peter Mountford, agrees that mothers have a harder time: "Jen is *always* wrong. At home with the kids, she's an anachronistic housewife; at work, she's ditching her kids to nurture selfish professional ambitions. Somewhere, lurking at the root of this all, is the tenacious idea that men *should* have a career, whereas women must choose between a career and being at home."[9]

Our culture still expects women to be primarily responsible for the children — and the household. I would add that if a mom stays at home, she's frequently viewed as a second-class citizen. I have heard of husbands saying they will "give" only 20 percent of their income to their wives because they don't contribute any earnings! And then I hear working women bemoaning that they still do most of the work to keep their household functioning; it is not shared 50/50 with their husbands.

According to the National Stay at Home Dad Network, SAHDs experience isolation and loss of identity because they are not leaving the house every day in obvious pursuit of a career. Stay-at-home-dads face commentary from men that misses the point: "Man, it must be nice to not have to go to work every day," "It would be nice staying home all day doing nothing," "Hee, hee! Got any good recipes?"[10]

Such comments also show what people think about stay-at-home-moms.

As we see, we are walking in some new parenting territory. Not only are the parenting dances changing, but who is in the dance and the location of the dance may differ. And the challenge of having time for ourselves isn't just affected by whether we do or don't work outside of the home. It also reflects a shift in how our children play. Rather than informal play among different age groups, the norm now is for children to get together more formally (scheduled and paid for) with their peers.

And sometimes it just reflects real life! Sally, a stay-at-home-mom whose child has difficult behavior challenges, says that she would get angry when she was frazzled, making the whole situation worse. And then she'd cycle through guilt and exhaustion. She spent a lot of her time anticipating challenges and how to deal with them. She also spent time trying to find the people and resources she needed to help her and her family cope.

Lenora talks about her part-time job, her additional role in the family business, the schedules of her two children, and managing the household. She would just get worn down and run on, well, coffee.

This "no time for me" seems to be more experienced by mothers, not that fathers don't ever experience it. Perhaps it's because working mothers are still likely to come home and make dinner, help the kids with homework, go out for groceries and so on.[11] And others often feel that stay-at-home-moms get enough time to themselves during the day.

Our motherhood time challenges are also affected by other cultural shifts — more hours of homework for our kids, and more school stress because of the push to get into college. College was not always considered a requirement for getting a job. Now a bachelor's degree is considered a must.[12] So our kids are stressed, and we are stressed with them. Have you ever noticed how stress affects your sense of time?

Part of our "no-time-for-me" feeling comes from our sense of what it takes to succeed in our culture. What do you think it takes to succeed? It seems we dwell more and more on how competitive it is for our children. Witness this pressure about getting into college. It starts in elementary school with talk about how competitive it is and how the best candidates not only excel in their classes but are also engaged in extracurricular activities. Children are told to be best, first, stellar and then some.

Whew! If you buy into this, you not only have a stressed household, but you won't have much time for anything other than pushing your child to meet these "requirements" for success!

In Lorna Landvik's novel *The View From Mount Joy*, a high schooler named Joey says this about how parents' role with their children has changed:

It seems there has been a shift in the family hierarchy; nowadays parents do everything for their kids. If junior's an athlete, his parents enroll him in expensive clinics and traveling teams and easily transfer him to a different school to give him a better playing opportunity. Hell, when we played, lots of parents didn't even come to regular games, saving their appearances for tournaments or playoffs. Not that we minded — our parents weren't on us the way parents are on kids now. But conversely, it was understood that in the family's decision making, the adults were the captains and the kids were second string, if they were even allowed on the team.

Today's dominant parenting culture is a driving force behind our sense of No Time for ME!

Dads feel it, too. David described how it stressed him when, on his first day at a new job, his son got sick and it was his turn to deal! At first he couldn't begin to think what to do. He froze and reports he literally kept running in circles. How do I take care of my very important work responsibilities and my very important son?

Since we are parenting in new cultural territory, we need parenting with new, intentionally developed skill sets. Reconciling our sense of "no time for me" with our need for self-care requires that we grow in our capacity to L.O.V.E.: to Listen to ourselves and surrounding influences, to drop into OM (calm and clarity), to Voice our sense of disharmony, to Visualize our values in action in a harmonic way, and to Explore our thoughts and hear the thoughts of others. We absolutely need time for ourselves to stay healthy.

If this is an issue for you, use it as the problem you focus on in the second part of the book. You will indeed find new solutions.

Sally, Lenora, and David enlarged their capacity for different parts of L.O.V.E. Sally and David increased their ability to drop into OM. Once Sally learned how to get into her OM space using listening and visualization, she found herself reacting from an inner calm and simply not engaging in the upset. She was able to connect to her love for her child. This had a profound effect on her and she was able to rearrange things in her schedule and find time for herself.

David remembered his favorite OM strategy (you will see much more on this in the OM Moment chapter), calmed down, and talked to his new boss from that place of calm. They approached both of their needs with flexibility. The boss said David could look at some orientation materials at home and let him know which activities he would need to participate in, whether in person or virtually. Through OMing, David cleared his brain to think about options instead of feeling as though he were up against a wall.

I have experienced this issue fully. Especially since I made a commitment that my home would be a place for kids to gather. And gather they did! So not only was my house forever lively, I also did a lot of the driving to and from shared activities. I needed to be able to refresh quickly (plus I am an introvert, so I need my down time).

Plus, I have a highly sensitive daughter; she's sensitive to different foods, to energy, to people. Dealing with all of this had me often feeling as though there was no time for me. There was only time for work, taking care of the house, and her.

Using higher levels of listening, holding OM Moments, and getting better at voicing my needs frequently saved the day for me. I had more than one teacher across these skills as I built my confidence in using them.

I had to realize that when I started getting irritated a lot, that meant that either my daughter had gone to another developmental stage and I hadn't caught up (changed my behavior to be in harmony with it), or I was overwhelmed and needed to step back and take care of myself. I could only do this through listening in to myself and then getting better at finding my quietude so I could see and hear the situation and her differently. First I had to pay attention to what was going on with myself and my listening abilities.

We have to get into all of this, though, if we are to go beyond feeling "there's no time for me." I also needed to develop my capacity for OM Moments to go beyond this theme.

OM is about your "space," within which you release from what was and what is next. It is an energy state. It occurs when you connect with your creativity, your highest self and beyond. It is the state of those in deep prayer, meditation, or release. However, OM Moments are inherently against the grain of our analytical, extroverted Western culture. They cannot be analyzed. They are your time to be with yourself.

Some would say it is a state that connects us to our divine. Others say it's when our brain waves move beyond beta (the wave frequency of our awake consciousness and reasoning). They reach alpha, theta, delta, or gamma frequency, depending on how deeply we are released from thought.

There are many ways to get into an OM Moment. It's not all about sitting down and meditating, as you will see later in the chapter on OM Moments. It is important, though, for modern-day parents who are struggling with "no time for ME" to become intentional with their OM Moment learning curve.

I have relied on my OM space when I have particularly chaotic days. Those days inevitably have a negative effect on how I am with my daughter. Tension gets my adrenaline flowing and, before I know it, I am fighting or fleeing. Either response means my body is hyped up and I am irritable. So OMing (OM as a verb), calms me down. It creates homeostasis (the state of a body that is biochemically harmonious).

There is no way we can be freely loving when we feel a lack of time or attention for ourselves. All of our parenting issues, not just this one, can detract from our nurturing, loving energy. This issue of not having enough ME time reminds me of an observation in Nancy Koran's *The Zen of Tennis* — that we always have more time to get to the ball than we realize.

Committing to Listening and OM Moments will help you take care of yourself in all areas of your life, even as you give a lot of time and energy to your children. You will find your time for you!

CHAPTER 6

WHAT HAVE I GOTTEN MYSELF INTO?

THIS DANCE IS HARDER THAN I THOUGHT!

Most parents have muttered this at some time during their children's toddler and teen years. This is very normal. Both toddlers and teens have limited memories, thinking skills, and emotional management abilities. This is because of massive brain development and hormone shifts, not to mention physical growth and new developmental tasks. Toddlers, whose job is to explore and discover, have few words with which to explain themselves when upset.

And have you ever noticed how forgetful and emotional teens are? They have words. However, when they face challenges, they are not connecting with thoughts. Instead, they're connecting to whatever reward or pleasure they seek (calm, love, freedom, camaraderie, independent decision-making etc.), because the brain centers for rewards are gloriously large during the teen years. And the brain center that helps us make sense of things (connect the dots) doesn't really develop much until age 18 or so. Both toddlers and teens are in vulnerable phases of their life. And just when they need affection and reinforcing strengths from us, we are at our wits' end wondering, what did I get into?

Many times when I ask parents to describe their teen years to me, they flash a knowing smile. Most of us remember how we felt about all kinds of authority during those years. Gosh, what a time! We are looking to express ourselves through our style, our flirtations, to announce ourselves to the world, to be noticed by those we want to be with or be like. It is a huge, noisy stretch moving us into beingness, separate from our parents. And that being leads to all kinds of doing.

How much from your teen years did you bring along with you into your adult life? My answer is, "Quite a lot!" My desire to talk to many kinds of people blossomed then, as well as my awareness and affinity for heart-informed people. And all of this while authentic womanhood stormily, but firmly rooted in me.

Could I have put any of that into words at that point? No. Because there wasn't anybody around until my college years who could begin to touch on the depth of my experience.

Some kids go through this period with relative calm. But most people I've met experience a true human storm during their teens. And that means parents are feeling disregarded, like their kids don't value anything they've done, and they're totally afraid for their kids' future! We mutter about how we can't say or do anything right, our kids do the opposite of whatever we ask, if they even remember that we asked! (Short-term memory is not the strong suit of a teenager.)

We don't feel we are even on the dance floor with our kids sometimes, so where is the parenting dance? Parenting through the toddler and teen years can be exhausting, arouse all your worries, and cause you to doubt your best intentions as a parent. "If I'd only known . . ." you mutter. Many times.

And yet, the toddler and teen years are great times for helping our kids connect to their being, not their doing. It's prime expansion time, when they're operating from a place of personal motivation, values, and personal accountability.

For toddlers, it might be, "Do you want to wear this or that today?" Or, "If you bite Missy rather than use your words, what do you think will happen?" For teens, it might be, "If you take your eyes off the road to text, how long are you not looking at the road? What can happen during that time?" Or, "If you want connection in your life, do you drink till you're dizzy with friends, or do you listen to what they have to say about dating?" Through all of this, they're exploring their personal motivations and values. The more you get to that, the stronger life becomes for them. Scary, yes?

As a parent who has been there, and been with many other parents through this, I know it is a very destabilizing time at home. With toddlers, once you get the hang of being around the mood swings, giving and explaining choices works very well. Maybe not right in the moment, but definitely over time. With teens, it takes more time, not less.

It all means you need to be intentional about practicing for the Love Zone dance. It takes patience to build your L.O.V.E. capacity, which in turn gives you the patience you need with your toddler and teen.

Teens can be deceptive, because it's easy to think they aren't paying attention. For instance, if you say, "No cellphones at dinner," but you jump up to get yours when it rings ("It might be work"), your not-paying-attention-teen will pull out her cell at dinner. Teens may be quiet, but they observe you and notice how you handle things as opposed to how you *say* to handle them. Yikes!

What does that require of us parents? We have to take the time to L.O.V.E. I spent a lot of time during those years sitting in a rocking chair I use for contemplating things! I'm not sure there was one capacity I used over another; they all came into play frequently.

When your young adult starts making wise decisions, thanking you for listening, speaking about their own challenges, you'll know you have done your job well and that taking the time to expand your capacities was worth it. You'll remember why you got yourself into this!

It's not just everyday toddler and teen issues that cause us to wonder what we've gotten ourselves into. Another time I see this come up is when a child has some kind of mental health diagnosis. Getting things done, being level-headed, or paying attention can be difficult for kids with ADHD, ADD, OCD, anxiety, depression, and so on. Which means, the dance of parenting is difficult. And there's an increasing percentage of children with mental health diagnoses. Dr. Amy Houtrow of Children's Hospital in Pittsburgh says that physical disabilities are down by 12%. Yet a National Health Interview Survey of affluent homes found an increase of 28.4% in childhood disabilities (this includes learning disabilities and mental health/behavioral disabilities).[13] Therefore, an increasing number of parents are facing challenges, saying, "If I'd know what I was getting into. . ."

Navigating psychological/social imbalances in our children requires us to engage in all of our L.OV.E. capacities very intentionally. Because, if we don't, we will be consumed, defensive, ashamed, and uncertain about our role. Plus, we'll be reacting from fear rather than love. When parents react from fear, they're likely to become passive or its opposite, engage in power struggles.

A mother I know related how her husband got into power struggles with their teen son, who had a few mental health diagnoses, escalating whatever conflict was already going on. She said she didn't know which one to respond to, so she wound up getting angry, which in turn made things bad between her and her son. She would get so frustrated she'd say mean things to him, even hit him, and then feel guilty afterward.

I asked her to review the most recent argument as though she were watching a video. She was to stop the video when she noticed that her feelings were affecting her physically. It took about two seconds. I wasn't surprised because I knew her to be a sensitive person, one who would be able to readily sense her "stuff" showing up in her body (it does for everyone).

She did a mental scan of her body and realized several feelings showed up whenever she anticipated an argument. First she noticed that anger was dominant. Then that flitted away and was followed by fear. That one stuck around, which wasn't surprising: Fear is frequently the ground right under anger.

The feeling of fear seemed to be located by her heart. The area felt heavy, "self protective," she said. Notice that she was not just using her ears to listen to herself! She was using sensation, even for the words that came to her. That's really good listening.

As she kept throwing out words describing what she was "getting," she paid attention to the heart-heavy feeling and realized that she wanted to stay in the Love Zone with her son when certain conflicts came up. Getting angry and engaging in battle just made his behaviors worse, and it didn't make her feel very good, either. She realized that she wanted to change their communication pattern out of love for herself, too. There had been so much going on in this family that her sense of self-respect was taking a hit.

All of that she got from listening well to herself. And she has been able to remind herself of this when she is tired, when teen conflicts have been flaring a lot, when her husband approaches the conflict differently. It gets derailed at times — let's face it, when we're tired it's harder to resist a knee-jerk reaction, or the desire to put it all on someone else. But she knows how to listen and get back to how SHE wants to be in the sometimes chaotic times that go along with having a child with a mental health diagnosis.

The great news is, this woman has found her relationship with her son improving, as is her sense of self as she navigates the conflicts with different words and a different attitude, as she keeps listening to herself. She is doing a heroine's dance! Does the diagnosis go away, change? No. But by changing her reaction, this mother's life did. And it was her decision, not someone else deciding how she should react. Yes, she read about and explored different professionally advised options. But decisions in the end were authentically hers. Her child's neurobiology was destined to remain the same. Interestingly, though, the more she could be in the Love Zone with her son, the more some of his negative behaviors lessened.

Mental illness diagnoses for children are on the rise.[14] There are many hypotheses to explain it, from diet to play habits, to reporting mechanism, to better diagnosing, to the effects on humans of electromagnetic fields. It is not my purpose here to wade through it all, but rather to help you, the parents, figure out what is best for your child when you notice behavioral changes and don't know what to do.

You might be tempted to "just give them a pill," but finding the right pill might not be that easy. Or you might not want to accept what's going on, and insist, "It just can't be." But it then persists and gets worse. Or you might worry that your child will incorporate illness into his or her identity

("I'm depressed," "I'm OCD," "I'm bipolar") and limit his or her options. (A good therapist will help your child see beyond a diagnosis.)

A mental/behavioral challenge is like any chronic physical illness. You go through periods of being overwhelmed, of pushing it away, of feeling anger or sadness, and of accepting it and learning to be in life with it. The dance of parenting doesn't stop though, does it (except to pause for those OM Moments that you are getting really good at)?

If you are having moments of disbelief about how challenging parenting can be, because you have a child with a neurobiological imbalance, and find yourself saying, "If I'd known what I was getting into," know that you are not alone. Parents have this feeling even when there is no neurological imbalance. When this feeling comes up, it's time to practice more of your parenting capacities! The Listening exercises will help you see how you can be helpful rather than obstructing the way to good solutions. The OM Moments exercises will help you determine the best course of action for right now. By Visualizing and Voicing, you anchor your path through this challenging time by focusing on what you want to be saying by the "end" (I use quotation marks because some of these issues don't end even though the childhood stage does). By exploring, you'll find that you are not alone and that there is no doubt a great option for your child.

CHAPTER 7

WORRYING

Many parents figure worry just comes with the territory. To some extent that is true; worry is a product of our caring. However, when I talk to parents who are worriers, I often hear a level of worry that is sucking the fun out of their life as a parent, distracting them from what they'd like to be focusing on, and keeping options and solutions from opening up.

Worry is fear. Fear about the future. Even if it's about something that already happened, the worry is about how it will affect the future. One mother said: "My son flunked eighth-grade English. What will that do to his chances of getting into college?" She stood there wringing her hands as she said it. This was a real concern to her.

And yes, the concerns are real! It's what we make of it that matters, though. What is fear? A mother mentioned that she had to hurry home because her 14-year-old son would be home soon and she didn't want him to cook anything on his own. She was worried he would set the house on fire.

Someone asked her, "Is he absent-minded or careless, or is this a fear of yours?" She said that it was a fear of hers. The same person asked her if she'd ever taught him to cook so she could observe if he is thoughtful or thoughtless about it. She admitted she'd never thought of that and decided to start the next morning.

Because of her fear over a reasonable concern, she had never thought to cook with him so she could teach him and observe how much of a risk he might be in the kitchen. She must have been ready for a solution, because she "got it" right away.

What a great example of how worry over something very everydayish, cooking, turned into fear and kept her from problem solving. It happens to all of us; that's why we need each other!

Fear induces fight (arguments), flight (not engaging) or freeze (avoidance). It's simply not conducive to problem solving. Instead, we argue about suggestions from other people. We say we'll talk about it some other time and never get to that conversation. We avoid activities that relate to the situation, saying we are too busy or too tired. We stop doing our part of the dance in parenting.

There are also not-so-everyday things that come up. Parents naturally worry about some big things: addiction, isolation, their child making a mistake that could alter their life in some profoundly negative way, not having enough money to support a child's interest. The list could go on and on. Does any of this sound familiar? My child:

- ✓ is shy. I worry about her constantly - that others will take advantage of her, or she could be bullied.
- ✓ acts up every time we have to leave in the morning, and I am on a tight schedule. Will he ever get this right?
- ✓ is always getting earaches, what does that mean? And it's getting hard to miss work to get to the clinic.
- ✓ is 13 and so moody. Is she bipolar? Is she using drugs? What drugs are kids using now, anyway?
- ✓ dresses so suggestively, just like all the "stars" she watches. She'll wind up pregnant at this rate, or having something horrible happen.
- ✓ wants my attention all the time, even though I buy him all these cool toys.
- ✓ is not turning out like I wanted him/her to. What have I done wrong?
- ✓ is watching porn!

The dilemmas go on and on. Kids are bombarded with a lot. *You,* parents, are bombarded with a lot. Yes, it's important to get answers, but first, you must find your way to stay in the Love Zone, to not be in toxic worry.

As a parent, it will be so valuable to you to become aware of your thoughts around the outcome of events in your child's life. LISTENING. And to label them as a worry. VOICING.

How do you know it's a worry? People say, "I'm not worried, I'm just thinking ahead." If you fear something is about to happen and you are planning how to respond, it isn't destructive worry, it's preparation. In this way, worry is like stress: There is good and bad stress. There is good and bad worry.

If you are holding your breath at all, however, you are into destructive worry. It doesn't mean it's unfounded. It only means you have to watch yourself as you deal with the situation.

You might be concerned your child's eating habits will cause him or her to gain too much weight. So you go out and buy healthy food and look for ways to make it tasty. But if you are holding your breath and twittering inside about whether this will work or not, you are worrying. And that worry is getting passed on to your child.

So, first, identify it to yourself. "I'm holding my breath about this meal because I'm really worried about my child's weight." Your child picks up on this and before you know it, you are saying things like, "Well, you're getting fat, and I'm worried." It doesn't help the situation at all! Even though it is very real and you are just being honest.

Second, accept it. Meaning, stay away from mentally/verbally beating up yourself for worrying or your kid for causing you to worry. Just say, "Oh, that's worry," with no judgment about whether its right or wrong.

This is hard to do! Especially when it is something that is important to you. Worry is a monster in parents' lives. We must find a way out of it once we are in it. A great activity to try (after naming it and accepting it for what it is, worry) is VISUALIZING.

A father told this story about how he actually used visualizing to resolve arguments between him and his fourteen year old son. They were working on a building project together, and all they did was argue! Which design was better, who should do what, which tool was best for the job, should they work on it today or later. Every issue resulted in an argument. The dad started getting very worried about what his relationship with his son would be like by the time his son was sixteen. Then one day it occurred to him, what do I want it to look like?

So he spent some time figuring that out. He laid it out as a vision and, like all good visionaries, he kept that vision "in front of himself" even when things weren't great. He found he didn't argue as much with his son, he asked him more questions, he admitted when his son had a good idea, and he asked his son to find some different ways to say things to dear Dad.

Now this father reports that by the time his son was fifteen, he had the relationship with him that he had envisioned for sixteen. Did he have to zip it at times, getting there? Yes. Did he always think it was going to work out well? No.

And there is the rub about visualizing. One needs to believe steadfastly in the vision and keep taking steps that move toward that vision. Even in discouraging moments. Any manager, strategic planner, dream fulfiller, athlete, musician knows this. And it's true for parenting, too. Remember that visualizing the future shapes how you respond to things now. If you are saving for a particular car and you've visualized buying it next year, that shapes what you do now when it comes to other claims to your income.

Worry can take you off the parenting dance floor. Or if you stay on the floor, it might make you stiff and unable to connect with your partner (your kids). Just saying "Don't worry" doesn't turn the mind off. So start with listening to yourself and realizing that you are worrying. Accept it (don't be judgmental), envision what you want, then move into OM and more listening. Throughout this, explore with other parents. Worriers, do NOT leave yourself alone with your own mind!

A significant cause of worry is culture. Pay attention to what cultural influences are rearing up (as we discussed in Chapter 2) that force you to expect things of your child that just aren't realistic given who he/she is.

One of the bigger underlying causes of parental worries is something not often talked about: our parenting vows. All parents make these vows, which have a more intense energy to them than promises, such as, "My child will have more opportunities than I did" or "My child won't have to worry about money." It can take a while before they are realized, though, and in the meantime, they can generate a lot of worry and reactivity in us.

Consider Liz, who had this ongoing argument with her 17-year-old daughter about college. Liz wanted her daughter to go, but her daughter said she did not want to. It was creating a lot of arguing between them. Liz would ask, "When are you going to check out colleges?" The daughter would become hostile and say, "Mom, how many times do I need to say, I don't WANT to go to college right away?" The arguments usually escalated into every complaint they had about each other. At one point, Liz yelled, "You are SMART, I want you to go to college! I want you to have an easier life than me." Her daughter hadn't understood her mother's vulnerability. And Liz had made a parenting vow that was at odds with her daughter's desires.

It turns out this vow underlay many of the very intense conflicts they had about boyfriends, her daughter's early pregnancy, what she did with her time. It was very normal for Liz to react as she did to these things. But it led directly to ferocious arguments from which neither could disengage.

Once Liz was able to see her vow and take care of herself in some ways, their conversations and ideas about options started to expand. We can't avoid that we have parenting vows. They are blooming throughout our lives. What we can do is approach them differently. So listen to yourself. Are you:

- ✓ reacting strongly but nothing is changing?
- ✓ worrying day in and day out and just can't seem to let go of it?
- ✓ always in conflict with your child and/or your parenting partner? Include grandparents and daycare providers or friends when you answer the parenting partner part of the question.
- ✓ finding yourself being critical, judgmental of your child or parenting partner (even if you don't voice it, it's there)?

- ✓ not saying something that you think needs to be said because you don't want conflict?
- ✓ feeling lethargic or stuck in your relationship with your children?
- ✓ "fixing" things for your children, thinking that "I'd better do this or some bad thing will happen to them"?
- ✓ frequently smoothing things out between your parenting partner(s) and your children?

If you answered "Yes" to one or more of these, rest assured you are not alone. And rest assured you are likely up against the intensely charged energy of a parenting vow of which you are unaware. Or, you might be aware but just don't know how to get out of the intense energy around it. (There is a useful, great parenting class at OMGparenting.com that explores what parenting vows mean.) [15]

A prospective father told me how nervous he was about the birth of his son because he was afraid of how their family finances would be affected. After some conversation, it became evident that he didn't want to argue about finances but they were extremely important to him. He wanted his child to learn about the issue "as soon as he can count." This might sound a bit over the top, but given his life experiences, it made sense. After we talked about parenting vows, where they come from, their positive and negative effects, he was able to label his vow and find ways to imagine it all working out.

It is so important, and not terribly difficult, to become aware of your vows. And once you do, you'll automatically become less stressed and have more fun.

Worry IS normal for parent. It is the degree, frequency, and pattern of the worry that matters. When it occurs every day, then it is time to give it attention. Believe it or not, you don't need to be worrying all the time! Or even half the time. Start using the L.O.V.E. practices from section two to relieve the burden of worry.

CHAPTER 8

AM I A GOOD PARENT?

WHAT ARE THE CRITERIA ON WHICH THIS DANCE IS JUDGED?

A sister to the experience of parental worry is the question, "Am I doing the right thing?" With so much often contradictory information on topics important to parents, so many choices for education, so much technology, so much of everything, it is easy to be uncertain. This kind of self-doubt is, to a degree, normal. How could we not second-guess choices when there are so many options and we feel the responsibility of leading our children along a path that will enhance their lives. It's like we're in a jazz dance about life's agony!

Uncertainty creates excitement, but also stress. Parents deal daily with managing emotions, determining if their child fits into developmental norms, budgeting sanely, managing their own lives, and just getting everybody where they need to be, on time. It's no wonder parents are stressed!

One Mom had just taken her one-year-old son in for his checkup. She told me the doctor had said the boy's speech was delayed and recommended speech therapy. She was feeling like an awful parent.

I asked if he was learning two languages, because it takes longer for bilingual children to use English words clearly at given milestones (they catch up by age 4 or 5). He wasn't. I asked a series of questions: Is he pointing to things when he wants them? Yes. Is he looking at books? Yes. If you ask him to find an object on a page, like an apple, does he point to it? Yes. Does he repeat sounds, like da-da or ta-ta? Yes. Does he play peek-a-boo or clap his hands if you ask him? Oh, yes. If you ask him to find something simple or do something simple with it, does he? Yes.

This child's speech was not delayed. As with all development, even among adults, a series of steps build toward the ultimate outcome. In this case, the doctor was concerned about the number of words the child knew. However, the boy was taking every step in speech development that leads to words. Knowing this was an attentive mother who could play with her son in a way that enhanced his development, I felt the words would simply come. We discussed some additional things the parents could do to help. And indeed the boy moved along just fine.

The point is that people, even people of great knowledge and authority, will tell you things throughout your parenting that might cause you to wonder if you are doing the right thing. And it's easy to jump to the conclusion that, if they say you or your child aren't meeting some standard out there, you are failing as a parent!

I asked this mom what she felt inside herself about her son's speech (Listening). Her sense was that he was fine. Dad felt the same. I encouraged her to go with that sense and believe it, to listen to herself. She wound up getting some pop-up books and ones with different textures (like *Pat the Bunny*) because they seemed to interest her son more. And he was indeed interested in those books and started learning more words. But meanwhile, she had been intensely exploring and questioning what was the right thing to do. She worried about whether she was a good mother.

Interestingly, the boy's father really wasn't concerned. He was confident they were already doing the right things and didn't give any more thought to it. It reaffirms for me the notion that our culture still places the responsibility for our children's success on women. In the same way, we still place the burden of financially supporting the household primarily on the men (they have an awful time when money is tight; above and beyond the practical aspects of how to fund needs, it affects their sense of manhood).

How do we know if we are doing the right thing? That we are doing everything we can do, that we're on track? Listening to yourself will give you the answer. Our inner voice never lies. Trust it! And if we could learn to listen to it better, we'd have less doubt and our relationships would feel more energized. We'd have a great sense of calm. This mother in fact felt her son's language development wasn't a problem. It was hard to trust, however.

As I said, it's pretty normal when we care as much as we do about our kids, to have moments of self-doubt. And self-doubt is not inherently a bad thing — we should indeed pay attention to "Are we doing the right thing?" But dwelling on it, letting it take over, acting from that doubt is very demoralizing and it will keep us from making the most constructive and energizing decision.

This boy's mother felt like she was a bad mom for a day or so, but because she was used to noticing her feelings and thoughts, she knew they have an energy of their own that can take over a situation (happily or unhappily so). She eventually returned to her usual confidence by Listening to herself, Voicing her concerns, Exploring options, and calming down enough (OM Moments) to observe everything more clearly.

Because of our caring, it's easy to fly into these moments of intense self-questioning. That's unlikely to stop. For instance, have you tried to sift through the information about:

- ✓ lactose intolerance? The doctor says, "Put her on soy formula." You have read that the way soy is processed is not good. What do you do?
- ✓ ADHD being diagnosed in children at three years of age? There is conflicting information about the suggested medications. Is the diagnosis even right, because others say all three-year-olds are ADHD? What do you do?
- ✓ the right way to talk to kids about traumatic news they have seen on TV?
- ✓ video gaming, good or bad?

Fortunately, we have a way to determine the right course of action: LISTEN in. When we don't, situations get worse. This mom's actions, and the energy emanating from them could have put pressure on her son to use words because she wanted to show that she was a good mom. Or she could have done the same because she feared her son would be behind others and suffer ridicule. But she truly wanted to help him grow at his own pace.

Have you noticed how your parenting mind works? Something you feel bad about occurs and in a nanosecond you're imagining your kid failing, struggling, and having a horrible life! We need to develop and trust that internal thermometer that tells us whether there is truly a problem or that things are really a-okay. That's Listening.

The need to Listen to ourselves is crucial in modern life. With so much information coming at us and a culture that is very focused on time and outcomes, it really is hard to know what to pay attention to. Even though there are lots of smaller outcomes, steps toward achieving the milestone, we tend to overlook them and admire only the final outcome. Those milestones do tell us what is good, what is success, which we all want for our children. But the truth is, there is a wide range of normal development. If a child makes many of the steps toward a milestone, but is up to three months off on one or two of them, he or she is no doubt fine. Find and encourage activities that will help development, and off you go.

The right answer in one family isn't necessarily the right answer for another, so it takes the full circle of L.O.V.E. to find your way out of this jazz dance of agony and back to your loving parenting dance.

And how do you know you're a great parent? Most of us start out parenting with ideas about our child's success and they turn into ways we judge our success as a parent. Most parents I talk to say they want their child to be:

- ✓ successful
- ✓ happy
- ✓ self-confident
- ✓ healthy
- ✓ in good relationships

When we say these things, images cross our mind. For instance, a report card filled with A's, a graduation ceremony, a son in a suit and an air of success, a daughter standing calm in conflict, a wedding. . . The images go on. These thoughts and corresponding mental images are consciously and unconsciously there from the day we say, "I'm pregnant." When you were expecting or in the early days of parenting, what thoughts and images crossed your mind when you thought about what you wanted for your child? They form your Vision of life as a parent.

This list, which is very normal to have, also marks the beginning of the stress. We wonder what we are doing wrong when our baby cries, when our son is depressed or our daughter anxious, when there are D's on the report card, when our toddler bops someone on the head or hides behind our legs, when our teen doesn't know whether college is for her or what she wants to do when she grows up. Before you know it, you feel like you are failing as a parent! And that affects your responses to what is happening in your child's life.

Where is your wish list coming from? What is your idea of parenting success? Are these ideals driven by your culture or your personal beliefs? What is the list you use to evaluate your success as a parent? Here is mine. It wasn't always this. It evolved over the years as I faced decisions that left me wondering, "Am I doing the right thing?"

I have decided that I am successful as a parent if my daughter:

1. expresses a wide range of emotions to me (even babies have a range of feelings)
2. explores the world with curiosity
3. consciously accepts or rejects norms
4. questions the limits I set
5. asks for help from me, teachers, friends, professionals
6. examines out loud the upside and downside of a course of action/ behavior
7. accepts or rejects a course of action because it is not true to her (or expresses that she will meet minimal requirements if it's a "must-do")

8. has a variety of friends because she pays attention to a person's character
9. struggles with showing sensitivity to others while also having her own feelings

How does this change your sense of success as a parent? And your mind's images, Vision, of successful parenting? What you think affects what you see, what you react to, and how you react. Thinking about your Vision of successful parenting is time well spent, because it will serve as a conscious guide in times of uncertainty. You move through this, and answering the question "Am I a good parent?" by using all of your L.O.V.E. capacities.

CHAPTER 9

UNDERAPPRECIATED

I THINK I'M DANCING ALONE

Sometimes as a parent it's pretty easy to feel that if you *are* dancing, you are definitely dancing alone. The other dancer is off doing their own thing and forgot the two of you are in this dance together.

Women are still largely feeling they have to do it all: parent, nitty-gritty household management, relationship management, and work (or if not working outside of the home, then they have to defend their daily accomplishments). This seems to be true for even partnered moms, not to mention the 26 percent of households headed by a single parent[16]. I also hear parents talking about how the kids don't understand "all that needs to be done; they just aren't helpful." According to a survey by Braun Research in 2014, 82 percent of grown-ups polled said they had regular chores when they were growing up, but only 28 percent reported asking their children to do any.[17]

It is natural for children to not appreciate all that it takes to run the home. For one thing, we tell them that "going to school is your job." They think our job is to keep their lives going.

It's surprising how much this also comes up between partners, whether under the same roof or in a co-parenting arrangement. It's not uncommon to hear parents complaining about how their spouses don't "get it," asking "What did you DO today?" The feeling of "I do it all" persists.

That stay-at-home-moms feel underappreciated is well documented, as is the fact that working moms feel they "do it all." Because stay-at-home-dads are now also expressing this, it seems our culture still places more value on earning money and maneuvering in the work arena than on overseeing a household budget and maneuvering through the logistics of family life. As a side note, Texas teacher and blogger Steve Nelms valued a stay-at-home parent's contributions at $73,960 per year in 2015.[18]

No matter what, feeling underappreciated can lead to a cycle of behaviors that truly run down a relationship, whether between parenting partners or parents and their children. Being underappreciated is very isolating in a relationship. To compensate, people fall into a passive response of overaccommodating or into an aggressive response of being defensive and negative. Either pattern represents a demoralized parent, which has a huge effect on the entire home.

Those who overaccommodate might have a variety of motivations, but typically they don't want to deal directly with feeling underappreciated so they start to do, do, do — to say okay to a lot of things they really aren't okay about doing. It might be driving the kids to yet one more activity, it might be preparing a meal for additional people who arrive by surprise, it might be constantly changing their plans so someone else's schedule works better.

Those who respond aggressively, also with differing underlying motivations, might sigh a lot or criticize their child or partner when asked to do something, or they might do what's asked but storm angrily about not being appreciated (passive aggression). This is so pervasive in households. How do we get out of this?

On a very practical level, it doesn't matter where or how you live, if you are a parent, you are involved in so many household responsibilities and activities, it gets confounding. Who "closes up" the house at night? Who puts the kids to bed? Who gets them going in the morning? Who plans meals and buys the groceries? Who plans summer activities? Who pays the bills? Who goes to the school to pick up the sick child or talk to the teacher? Who makes the doctor appointments? Who takes the kids to the clinic? Who cooks? Who takes the car in for an oil change? Who packs for vacations? Who does the laundry? Who goes with the kids to buy clothes? Whose work is more valued?

The list goes on and on. The first step to smoother household management is to acknowledge that these duties and chores exist and then assess how they're distributed. It's an interesting exercise. And it's necessary if you are exhausted and underappreciated.

In Appendix A, you'll find a questionnaire that you can use to take an objective look at how household responsibilities and chores are distributed. Use it with your partner, whether you are working outside of the home or not. Use it with your tweens and teens to reallocate your load. There is space for adding your household's unique requirements to the list.

So now that you have acknowledged that there is a problem, that you feel underappreciated, what do you do? One mom, Mimi, had a hard time at first hearing that she was being underappreciated, that her over-accommodation was affecting her! It's pretty easy to feel this way as a parent because, after all, it is a very giving kind of role. Mimi had to start to Listen to her own frustration and see where it was showing up for her. She was surprised to discover how tight her muscles were from holding in her anger. She was gradually able to look at specific situations and envision how they would be different if she were appreciated (Visioning). Once she got to that, she was able to start to change her responses when she felt this.

It was a bit different for Tosh. She complained that her two-year-old son was ridiculously demanding and never helped out. She was fast to cut down her husband for how he cleaned the kitchen, was tight with money, and didn't understand much of anything in her world. Taking one issue at a time, she came to realize how she was feeling underappreciated and therefore critical of almost everything they both did. Her sense of being underappreciated did not start in her current family life, hence her tension around it all. Once she started to see the layers of this feeling within herself, she was able to start to calm herself (OM Moments) and find different responses (Explore and Voice).

Once the problem of not being appreciated is acknowledged, the way through it is to use the L.O.V.E. strategies suggested in Section Two of this book. One person's solution will be different from another's because all people and homes are unique.

Being underappreciated means you feel powerless, which can take you deeper and before you know it, you've lost your sense of self-worth. You need to admit it, to yourself at least. Then you can start to shift, to take pride in your value, and the world will start to shift as you find different responses to requests coming your way. You will be able to move out of overaccommodation or aggressive defensiveness and back into the dance of parenting. Using your L.O.V.E. capacities will ease your transition into being fully appreciated.

CHAPTER 10

VULNERABILITY TO EXPANSION

I'VE GOT SOME NEW MOVES

The previous chapters have focused on parenting challenges. We come and go from them, and occasionally we get stuck. However, all is not bleak. For one thing, you can get unstuck. For another, by looking at ourselves in our parenting challenges, we get better at life! And that is what the rest of *The Dance of Parenting* is about — how you find your inner choreographer who will ALWAYS get you back in the dance, with some new moves.

It is through relationships and our response to life that we heal, or not. What is healing but strengthening and opening a heart that has shut down and retreated from pain? Our children open us up as few things in life do. So what better relationship is there to allow ourselves some more heart and mind growth?

The first few months after my baby was born, I felt a sense of joy that I hadn't even known existed before then. When she looked at me with those innocent, concentrating baby eyes, wow! When she started to laugh, wow! It was like my spirit soared on that laughter. My parenting dance was full of leaps, glorious twirls and great lifts.

That intense opening of my heart led me to pay attention to joy in other parts of life. And my life has steadily opened up to trusting and sustaining joy. I have also become more accepting that joy isn't the totality of my experience in life; being down or angry doesn't take away from the joy or make it something to be wary of.

This has been a great gift of parenting to me. When I was a child, I experienced joy. I was one of those kids for whom everything was made right by a beautiful day. That feeling was interrupted by some problems around me, plus I was seen as missing a lot of the meat of life because I could be so joyful. I reconnected with my spirit through this gift of parenting. Now I get to have joy along with everything else I experience in life. I say, "Thank you, thank you for the gifts of parenting."

To get these gifts, one has to be open, listening (noticing), and vulnerable. If I wasn't open to more joy, it wouldn't have happened. If I didn't listen to myself, I wouldn't have known it did happen! The joy was great, yet all my learning wasn't out of joy; some of it was out of my vulnerabilities. Parenting makes every single parent vulnerable, but I've noticed parents hate to admit that!

Vulnerability in parenting shows up in the things that stress us, the things that worry us. When our 10-year-old has three things they want to do after school, and we are stressing about how to pay, how to schedule it all, how to give them the life they want, we are vulnerable! We think it's our kid's vulnerability we are stressing about: what if they don't do this, will it diminish their opportunity to get into college, will it make them lonely because all their friends are doing things, will it make them feel different because their family can't support these activities? All very loving concerns. But we, the parents, are also vulnerable about our ability to provide.

One definition of vulnerability is being susceptible to harm, feeling that someone or something is threatening us in some way. Another definition is feeling open to criticism or moral attack. As parents, that could come from teachers, other parents, our kids. Or worse yet, ourselves! It's a very unpleasant feeling.

Vulnerability as a parent is the antithesis of what we're supposed to feel, after all. We're supposed to be in the lead, in the know, in command. A cultural myth. We are willing to talk about worries and stress, but not vulnerability. Yet can you really love without also feeling very vulnerable? We acknowledge that in romantic relationships, even friendships. But we need to take the step into acknowledging it as being part of our parenting experience.

When we see our vulnerability, voice it, and have the courage to own it, that's when parenting gives us the gift of expanding our lives. I could hardly write about vulnerability without mentioning author and Professor Brené Brown, who says, "Vulnerability is the birthplace of love, belonging, joy, courage, empathy, and creativity. It is the source of hope, empathy, accountability, and authenticity. If we want greater clarity in our purpose or deeper and more meaningful spiritual lives, vulnerability is the path."[19]

I'm thinking of the parents I've talked with as I write this. They've expressed feeling vulnerable about the following and more:

- ✓ financial worries
- ✓ not having a college degree
- ✓ getting laid off a job
- ✓ having trouble getting to work on time due to public transportation
- ✓ a sickly child
- ✓ a child with a mental health diagnosis
- ✓ a parenting partner who isn't supportive
- ✓ constant conflict with a child
- ✓ a child with an addiction
- ✓ a child not succeeding in school, on the sports team, in the dance troupe, etc.
- ✓ managing work and home
- ✓ taking care of the pets
- ✓ views that differ from community norms

As you can see, it's the stresses and worries of life that leave parents vulnerable. Let's get the gifts of that vulnerability! How? By Listening to yourself, Voicing it, Exploring it, and using your OM Capacity to go deeper with it than just saying "I'm stressed" and getting agitated or avoiding and blaming everyone else for it.

You must have the courage to own your vulnerability to get its gifts. Owning it is owning yourself. And when you own something you love (imagine owning your favorite car), you take care of it and ask how to do that if you don't know, you talk about it, you feel horrible if something threatens it and you look for ways to protect or sustain it, you go all out for it. So do this with yourself as a parent, too! Own all of your parenting experience, even your vulnerabilities.

When my daughter first seemed like she might have depression, I did not own my vulnerability around that for about a year. I was afraid for her. I was totally uncertain how to deal with it. I felt I had failed somewhere that she could feel so low. I basically shut down over it.

I must have been doing some breathing around it, though, because I finally said, "I'm scared." I was scared of her being harmed, which would harm me. I was scared she'd get a wacko therapist. I was scared of being criticized for something about my parenting.

Amazing things happened when I voiced what I was hearing in myself. My daughter and I talked about what would feel good to her if she was seeing a therapist. I explored options, found three professionals, phone interviewed them and the one that sounded good to me over the phone in fact got the job after we all met! This led to so many good things, not just for my daughter but also for me. I didn't feel so alone in parenting, so my energy increased. I learned a lot about teenage life, so my understanding of child development grew. I affirmed that good people are available for help, so my sense of security in life strengthened. My understanding and love for my daughter expanded, because I wasn't reacting from a shutdown heart and mind.

Don't get me wrong, these wonderful life expansions didn't happen overnight! Things that are significant to us, like loving our children, require cycles and cycles of L.O.V.E.

And guess what, everything I learned, she learned, too. What do we always say? That our children learn about life by observing us and how we deal with its challenges. So my gifts became her gifts. And she has taken them and flown with them.

Not all vulnerabilities show up over something major. Sometimes it's in everyday things that look like something else. I'm thinking of a mother who was often angry at her daughter. They had lots of fun times, but she always felt that her daughter was doing this and that all wrong. It was years later that she realized she felt perpetually vulnerable because she'd been criticized throughout her growing-up years. So, when her daughter didn't comply, got sassy, was forgetful, it touched on all that vulnerability. Their relationship became so challenging that the daughter disengaged from the mom when she reached twenty, letting her know that it was because of her constant anger. The mother wound up opening up to that and taking care of herself. They have subsequently re-engaged and are experiencing an expanding relationship. Bravo to both of them for having courage! L.O.V.E. is at work, listening to self and to each other, calming down if something gets triggered (using an OM Moment). Now they both hold a vision of how they'd like their relationship to be. They are both voicing their needs and exploring this new territory with openness. Both of their lives are expanding and a new confidence is evident.

Remember that your parenting vulnerability is a great time to practice L.O.V.E. Ironically, it is when we face our vulnerability that we find our strength and receive the greatest gifts of parenting. It's a beautiful thing!

On this note, move on to Section Two and find practices that will help you use your natural capacities of L.O.V.E. As author Belinda Luscombe says about all the research done on happiness in parenting: "Parenting makes you happier. Parenting makes you unhappier. Having children expands the continuum of emotions a human is able to feel."[20] In other words, you might as well get on board with it and let it work for you so it can work for your children.

SECTION TWO

GETTING BACK IN STEP

FINDING YOUR INNER CHOREOGRAPHER

We all get out of step when parenting. We have an off day, our children throw us a curve ball, or life just happens. We get to be out of step! But for the dance to go on, we need to get back in step or find a new step. That's the focus of this section: how to get back in step by finding your choreographer within. This section is about growing your parenting capacities so you are rockin' your parenting dance!

Each of the capacities is discussed, practices for strengthening that capacity are provided, and how this capacity might look in everyday life.

There are a few ways to approach this section.

1. Simply move into the practices as they're arranged here (in text boxes) and note your experience.
2. Have a specific parenting challenge in mind as you move through each chapter.
3. Pick the capacity that seems right for you to work on at the time. You will eventually get to all of them because they loop together, making a ring.

Any approach works. You can't OM without LISTENING. There's a lot of EXPLORING in finding a new way to address an issue that has come up through your LISTENING. It's easiest to decide on an approach if you have a VISION. And when you LISTEN, OM, and VISUALIZE you are going to *want* to VOICE!

Keep reminding yourself this isn't about perfection. It's a dance, and since it's about parenting it's forever new! We get to keep at it, accept our good and bad days. We gradually get better and better at more easily getting back in step when we get out of step. We gradually improve at getting back in step when we get out of step. You'll find yourself managing the dance with greater success. And what a difference that makes!

So what is your challenge? I assume you identified it because this situation and/or your response to it is bugging you. Good for you — you are already listening to yourself!

CHAPTER 11

LOVE'S "L" CAPACITY - LISTENING

What do you do when you hear,

- "You aren't listening to me!"
- "I just want to do it my way"
- "You said yes when I asked you, so why are you saying I didn't ask you?"

What do you do when you can't figure out for the life of you what is going on with your son, daughter, partner?

What do you do when you are unable to focus, are feeling irritated a lot, just can't seem to get something right?

What you can do is stop, and listen.

> The first duty of love is to listen.
>
> Paul Tillich

Listening is actually noticing with all of your senses yourself and the other. Seeing the expression on the other person's face, hearing the sound of their voice, feeling the way the air is moving around your skin, the scent, the taste . . .

WHAT DO YOU LOSE IF YOU DON'T DEVELOP THE "L" CAPACITY?

When you don't listen

- ✓ discussions go round and round or escalate
- ✓ your actions frequently make situations worse
- ✓ there is no chance for real healing
- ✓ there is no chance for the absolute best solution to arise

Think of times when your partner or child didn't listen to you, and you will know exactly what this means! You could probably make a very personal list of what happens when they don't really listen to you. In fact, go ahead and do just that; what happens to you and what happens to them?

WHAT DO YOU GAIN BY DEVELOPING THE "L" CAPACITY?

I get excited just looking at this list of what listening brings!

- ✓ better understanding of what and why
- ✓ new solutions
- ✓ a complete sense of calm and comfort, inner peace
- ✓ healing
- ✓ relationships that feel energized
- ✓ an internal "thermometer" to let you know when there's still heat in the situation or whether it has cooled off
- ✓ feeling happy about the resolution
- ✓ a realization that thoughts and feelings have energy

Listening is now part of teaching curriculums for business, counseling, and communications. But there is no curriculum to teach parents how to listen! Until now that is.

LISTENING 101

If you are new to listening or you just want to have some fun with it, use this sensing practice. Sensing is at the center of listening. And there is no better place to start with listening than sensing yourself, because that is the basis of not just Listening, but of OMing and Visualizing.

Exercise #11.1: Sensing

1) What do you notice in your body?

2) Where do you notice tension or feel that your breath isn't reaching?

3) Who else is in that area of tension with you (other than whomever you are having the conflict with)?

4) What are they saying to you?

5) What do you feel they are saying? i.e. do you feel left out, alone, scared, threatened, not good enough?

This all feels rather negative, but honestly, we don't get tense when we feel love, kindness, understanding, or confidence.

Bodies talk, and very honestly. Wondering what that tight muscle is honestly telling you, when you sense it isn't about exercise? Sometimes you'll know right away. Sometimes you won't, but the process will get faster once you learn to *listen to your body*, and get over how strange a thing that might seem.

LISTENING 102:

Once you're using your Listening 101 skills without even thinking about it, think of the situation you chose to pay attention to. It's okay, even best, to do this if you aren't actively in the situation that is challenging you. You get to practice while reflecting on it. Over time, you'll do it while *in* situations. For now, with your challenge:

Exercise #11.2: Tuning In

1) What sounds do you hear, and what are they saying to you about this situation?

2) What expressions do you notice, and what do they tell you?

3) What muscles feel tight as you think about it? Just scan your body.

4) What is the overall feeling you had from the other person's communication?

When we talk, we absorb a lot of information from what we are hearing — not just the words but *how* the words are said. My father always said, "It's not *what* you say but *how* you say it." Plus, there could be other sounds and expressions that are giving you information. So now, think about your situation. What else are you hearing?

Exercies #11.3: Sensing and Tuning in Together

1) Focus on an area of your body where you are feeling tension.

2) Breathe gently "into" that area, just picture your breath going there. Keep breathing until you feel air moving through the area.

3) As the air starts flowing, ask, What are you telling me?

4) Sometimes you'll instantly get an idea about what might be causing your tension, sometimes it will come to you later. But you will start to "hear" what you need to pay attention to.

The interesting thing is that we do not always accurately interpret what we hear when listening. We assume we are accurate, so the next part of this exercise is to *check out your assumptions*. You have heard the expression that to assume makes an ass out of you and me? For instance, you might be annoyed by the sound of pots and pans clanging in the kitchen and get angrier thinking that your child is ignoring your yells to stop. So, be more like a detective, setting assumptions aside: Go into the kitchen and say something like, "It seems like you are having a great time." Or if you think they are angry, say, "It seems like you are angry."

This isn't always easy, because when we are angry, we're likely to judge another's behavior negatively. And that makes us angrier! For example, when you come home annoyed about the traffic and your son ignores you, you might avoid him because you think he is angry at you for something, when in fact he was thinking about an interaction with a friend. And the fact that you kept your distance hurts your son. So he gets ornery. And round and round it goes.

The good news is, it can be sorted out! All it takes is a little listening and assumption checking.

Sometimes your own body is telling you to pay attention to something. Maybe after you resolve the miscommunication with your child, you notice your jaw muscles are tight. Is that because you are still angry? Is it because you chewed too hard on your meat at dinner yesterday? And did you do *that* because you were angry? Or is it because you are overwhelmed with having so much to do between your own stuff and your kid's stuff?

Remember, listening takes time. And practice. How weird is that? It is about using your senses while communicating, listening between the lines, and knowing more fully what is affecting you. Why is it so challenging? Move on to *Listening 103* and you will be saying, "Aha, I get it." But first, congratulations! You are developing some great core strength in this parenting capacity by using your senses more for listening!

LISTENING 103

Triggers . . .

As a parent, there will be times when you find yourself responding to things in a nonconstructive way; you've been "triggered," your buttons have been pushed! This is because of how you heard things and used your listening before, even back when *you* were a kid. It is all very normal! Yet it becomes a problem when it interferes with a harmonious adult life. And having a family that's off kilter because of a listening problem can affect your harmony greatly.

This is where listening gets really juicy. It is also where there is the greatest opportunity for energizing and expanding your listening, therefore your life.

Let's back up in time a bit. You were once a young child, a baby. As a baby, you had a ginormous sensory system, allowing you to feel and absorb everything going on around you. Everything you experienced was felt and interpreted through your senses. And very immediately. No words. So, if you felt hungry and were fed lovingly by someone, you felt full, warm, and happy. If people around you were tense, you felt tense and uncertain.

You then started to develop words and became pretty proficient by age three. Depending on how you grew up, you learned words for different feelings, and people around you acknowledged them. "I'm sorry you are sad/frustrated/impatient" or "It looks like this is so much fun for you!" Those kinds of comments helped you notice yourself and others. But still, even at three, the world had an awful lot going on that you could only watch, sense, and draw conclusions from that affected how you saw yourself and others.

If a dog bit you, all dogs were scary, not just that dog. If your parents fought over how to dress you, dressing became unpleasant. If everyone laughed when you made a mistake, you figured it was funny to make mistakes. If blonde girls always took toys you didn't want them to play with and nobody was around to intervene, you just might have developed a thing about blonde girls!

And such is the case until you are around six. By then your brain has developed enough so that you start to be a bit analytical. Your brain now is beginning to take in and interpret information. You can see why one thing is okay for me and another isn't. Or that this blonde is trouble when it comes to my toys, but the other blonde isn't.

The brain is very efficient at developing pathways between your feelings about an experience and your actions. So, when you are hungry, you eat. If dogs scare you, you either reflexively keep your distance or are aggressive when you see one. If your parents fought over what you wore to school, you might get a knot in your stomach when it's time to go somewhere. You might respond to slip-ups with jokes if your mistakes as a toddler made people around you very serious. If your rotten experience with the blonde girl on the playground was significant enough, you might be defensive around blondes as you grow up. These reflexive responses may continue throughout your life until you understand that they aren't helping.

The timing of such experiences affects the future outcome a lot, although it need not be permanent.

The point is not that events give you predetermined responses. It is that all of us are born into a world where a lot is going on and our responses to it are immediate. Our brain is forming patterns for feeling and responding to events from the get-go. It is because of this that our subconscious mind becomes highly developed between birth and ages five to six.

There is a bundle of nerves in your brain that houses your subconscious feelings, which become your driving force. It's called the RAS – reticular activating system. It is very busy during the first five or so years of your life, storing information about how you feel and respond and responses you can anticipate. This is all prior to your ability to discern subtleties, do reality checks, or engage in critical thinking. In the RAS you have stashed all your automatic filters: what's important, what should be avoided, what should be handled aggressively, what shames you and what you do with that, what you trust and how you move toward it. In other words, this is one powerful center! Its job is to protect you so that you don't have to focus in detail on the ton of information you bring in every hour; it filters what YOU need and don't need, according to what your young self "decided."[21] It carries on in your life, driving your adult life, including your relationship with your children.

It is from this that early on, and throughout life, we develop beliefs about situations or people that can become self-limiting or self-enhancing. Why is all of this important to you in parenting? Because you bump into your own beliefs when things get "stuck" in life, including in parenting. You are likely bumping into something to do with RAS thinking, reacting patterns when you notice yourself

- ✓ saying the same thing repeatedly,
- ✓ getting worried about the same thing repeatedly,
- ✓ becoming irritable with your children a lot,
- ✓ feeling judgmental about your child.

It's possible your response comes from a belief that no longer works for you. If you are arguing repeatedly with your seven year old about wearing matching socks, you might believe that you have to look a certain way for people to take you seriously. But your child might see wearing unmatched socks as a great conversation starter when meeting other kids. Arguing about it not only adds unwarranted stress, but might also keep your child from opening up some valuable connections with you and others.

There are times in parenting when reaching out for support is very important, but do you deny yourself that option? It could be you think that is for weak people and you want to be the pinnacle of independence and creative problem solving. When you aren't having fun with finding creative solutions to a problem, take a look at the messages you got when you were young about needing support. Or at the messages you got about the very thing that you are upset about. Or the frustration you feel (like feeling ignored, underappreciated, not up to the challenge — all those topics in the first section of the book).

The next set of listening practices is to help in those times when you are getting nowhere with your son or daughter and you want to get unstuck. In the process of listening in, you might just bump into some of your beliefs that are guiding your knee-jerk reaction, intense feelings, or verbal monologues. None of which are helping you or the situation.

First, you aren't a "good" or "bad" parent because this is happening! It simply is the way life works! For all of us.

Remember, learning about and conquering our "triggers" is where the greatest opportunity for everyone's liberation and growth can occur. And it is actually fun! Our brain can change based on new experiences,[22] and listening gives us a way into the new.

You are good at noticing what is going on with your senses. Because you have practiced that. You are good at checking in about your interpretation of your senses. Because you have practiced that. Now you are going to get good at noticing what you are seeing/hearing in your mind's eye.

When you are NOT in the middle of a tension spot, think back on when you were.

Exercise #11.4: Knowing your triggers

Stop talking. Tune into the sounds outside. What different sounds are you hearing?

What feeling would you put to those sounds? Happy, sad, annoying, uplifting . . . ?

Stop talking. Notice the expressions on the faces of those around you.

What feelings do you think you are seeing? Puzzlement, frustration, gladness, warmth . . . ?

Stop talking. Notice the muscles throughout your body.

What is relaxed? What is tight?

Keep at this until you don't feel anyone with you in your body's tense area. What is the feeling you house there? That is a belief you acquired somewhere before you were five or six.

Congratulations! You have done exceptional listening to yourself.

A lot of times just listening like this will break up the old belief. But sometimes the belief is so potent that it won't break up right away.

This practice also tunes you in to how much energy your thoughts and feelings have! What you notice when you listen with your senses is their energy. And that is why we need patience, what I call here OMing.

LISTENING AND EVERYDAY PARENTING LIFE:

I remember well the college communication course in which I first learned about listening. At that point, nobody had talked about listening as a part of communication. I found it very exciting, in part because it turns out I did a lot of it! It was so good to learn it was an "art," and that there was a process, and that there was a term for what I did naturally (actually, all of us do).

It explained so much about what was happening to me when I was observing (another thing I do a lot of). I was noticing nonverbal expressions and myself! It in fact made me a powerful communicator, although I didn't think of myself that way; mostly my culture acknowledged talkers (it still does, although there are some shifts occurring). I started to notice others who listened similarly. Books started to be written about the subject in a way that brought it into the work arena more.

With the passage of time, I came to respect my listening more. I saw that what one could do with listening was limitless, and that I was limited in how I used this "tool." Subsequent to that college course, this has probably been one of my most fascinating life's learnings: my ongoing expansion of my capacity to listening.

And what challenged this capacity the most was, you guessed it, parenting! Not just the listening to another, but the listening to myself also.

When my daughter was a newborn, listening to her was so easy. Babies don't communicate with words. They are full of nonverbal cues, turning their head away from you when they've had enough of you, looking at you oh so intently when they can't get enough, clenched fists when tense, relaxed hands when at ease, rapid breathing when excited. The list goes on.

As parents, we quite naturally listen to babies with other senses too. And we talk to them about what we observe. "Oh, you like looking at that blanket." "What's going on, baby, what are you trying to tell me?" Of course, postpartum depression, a challenging co-parenting relationship, or work hardships can throw off even this baby phase of parenting.

It was easy to listen to myself too, during the baby phase: the mind boggling joy, the pleasure over every progression into the next milestone, and feeling the powerful connection from attunement to my baby.

Listening in the early stages of parenting can be rewarding. Later on it can become more challenging. Looking back, I'd say that it is very natural for us to put ourselves aside during the heavily dependent stage of infancy. It's highly supported by those around us. Then, as baby progresses, so too does life for the parents. We move into the ongoing rub of growing our lives while growing our toddlers through teens! It takes TIME to listen when we just want to react. I started to experience parenting challenges. I've learned that feeling challenged is the first cue that it's time to listen!

When we are in relationships, listening goes beyond just listening to the other person. It also means listening to ourselves. Listening is far from passive; there is a lot going on within. Sometimes that's easy – for example, my daughter wants to leave a bit later, so I look at my schedule and also check within to see if it is okay with me or not. Oftentimes this was not a snap assessment. It took time to question: How am I reacting? Why? What have I bumped into within?

I think we can all relate to those times we don't want to listen because we feel we deserve to be listened to! And as a mother or father, a week of living can sure get you there.

For me the challenges, and my ultimate life opening and expansion, centered around themes that were carryovers from my early years: how much caring is too much (boundaries), where is this energy coming from (intuitiveness and boundaries), am I doing enough (co-dependency), is this, that, or the other thing going to set her up best for the future (worrying). Your themes might be different. This sequence on the Listening capacity can help you determine your themes.

Activated in real-life scenarios, as are all of our themes, I simply had to explore how to listen to my child if I was going to live in a way that was connected to the energy and optimism that my self needs to thrive. It constantly took me outside of the box I contained myself in as a young person. My world expanded so much through learning to listen differently and more deeply. That is such a gift I have been given through being a parent. And it's still happening, even with her being a twenty-something.

CHAPTER 12

THE "O" CAPACITY - OM MOMENTS

Dynamic Equilibrium!

(a phrase borrowed from math that describes OM Moments)

Strengthening your capacity for OM Moments is about getting still *within* yourself (you can be running and be OMing, and, yes, I'm using it as a verb). You have to intentionally do certain things to bring on a more balanced state within your body, mind, and spirit. It is a great place, so it's worth it!

When you give yourself OM Moments, you positively affect your response to a challenge — physically, mentally, emotionally, and spiritually — as well as the overall energy of the challenge. Wow! Your body's homeostasis (balance) is enhanced. If your heart is racing or beating hard, it calms, returning to normal. If your digestive tract is sluggish or hyperactive, it returns to balance. If your mind is running, unfocused, sluggish, or stuck, you bring it around to calm, focused, energetic and working for you rather than against you. If you feel scattered, angry, judgmental, or anxious, an OM Moment can calm you.

Meditation is commonly connected to OM. And there is no doubt of its value. You can also achieve this homeostasis thru exercise/movement. Laughing, playing, listening to music, and petting your pets also create homeostasis. The key is that you focus on what you are doing as described in the following practices, and that you get the feel of the activity. OM is not a mental activity.

So much of parenting is mental: scheduling, organizing, thinking about what is best. OM Moments are meant to be a nano-vacation from all of that.

WHAT DO YOU LOSE IF YOU DON'T DEVELOP THE "O" CAPACITY?

If you think, this isn't for me, or I can't do those calming things, I don't have time, I can't sit still . . . you risk:

- ✓ losing health
- ✓ remaining stressed
- ✓ losing out on your best solutions from your most amazing creativity
- ✓ being angry, irritable, distant, losing yourself during life's storms (which affects your children)
- ✓ feeling disconnected from whatever you call your highest source
- ✓ experiencing diminishing returns in relationships with your kids

I know these aren't what you want, or you wouldn't be reading this.

> The amount of information that an average person is exposed to in a day is the same as a person from the 15th century was exposed to in his lifetime.
>
> Rick Smolan

The OM capacity helps us deal with the stress that keeps our whole self from flowing: physical, mental, emotional, and spiritual blocks. The biochemistry of stress affects just about everything: muscle tension, brain and immune system changes, even our ability to think clearly. All you have to do is scroll down Wikipedia's very good explanation of stress to see that. [23]

The current emphasis on data and information is beginning to affect parents. Just one example is Sproutling, a wearable baby monitor that records a baby's heart rate, skin temperature, motion, and position, and uses the data to determine her mood, comfort, sleep pattern, and even predict when she will wake up.[24] It sold out rapidly. Access to so much information may soothe you. But it also might hype you up.

WHAT CAN YOU DO?

OM a bit.

Much has been researched about the positive effects of getting into that alpha or theta state of meditation.[25-26]

Our everyday conscious awareness is called the beta state. When we sleep, ideally we slip into the delta state. Alpha, a step up from beta, is when the mind is relaxed, calm, even meditative. Theta, one up from there, occurs when we are in a creative, insightful mode or deeper meditation (no wonder artists can seem spacey!).

By developing your capacity to OM, as it's used in this chapter, you learn to get your parenting self into at least the alpha state rather quickly. And what a difference it makes in a day (you'll hear more about that in the last part of the chapter)! Some of the following practices will also help you get into a theta state, where you will gain insight into what your child needs, or what you do. So carry on!

WHAT DO YOU GAIN BY DEVELOPING THE "O" CAPACITY?

You get to do some things that create calm within your being. It's a part of what "take a deep breath" or "count to 10" is about. You acquire easy access to:

- ✓ valuable mini (or maxi) breaks (from something that has your pants in a bundle, your nostrils flaring, or your body unable to stay still),
- ✓ perspective on things that seem monumental but aren't,

73

There are many ways to naturally get into a meditative state:

Walking
Running
Laughing
Viewing....

That's the beauty of feeling present moment.

✓ recognition and neutralization of negative physical reactions, thoughts, feelings and whatever else is charging around within you,
✓ new ways of being with a challenge, reacting to it, solving it.
✓ more energy.

You don't need to be able to sit in a particular position, or empty your mind of thoughts and feelings, or even devote a lot of time to do this.

As I mentioned before, science has shown that meditation increases positive emotions, social connection, improves attention, increases brain volume in areas for emotion regulation and self-control, decreases stress, and increases your perspective and wisdom. MRIs of brains taken during meditation have showed increased grey matter in the frontal lobes and hippocampal areas, which results in positive emotions and emotional stability.[27] EEGs show that meditation increases electrical brain activity in the theta and alpha states. It's also been shown to increase levels of empathy (and don't we ever need that with our children!). OM Moments are about getting these benefits whether through official sit-down meditation or the other truly enjoyable ways we can achieve this alpha or theta state throughout our day.

Now, on to the practices that will help you get there!

OM 101

Body connect . . .

You can create OM Moments simply by focusing on your body. Start by noticing how you feel physically now. Check up and down your body.

Exercise #12.1: OM Moments 101

1) Breathe regularly.

2) While doing so, notice your body. Find its calm place and just breathe.

3) Keep breathing until you are ready to release from it.

4) If you can't find your calm place and feel that everything is charged up, then pick a place in your body, notice how it feels, and then breathe "into" it (breathe with your mind's eye focused on that spot as though you are routing your breath right to it).

5) Notice how that part of your body starts to feel like air is in fact moving through it.
    Keep doing this until you feel calm.

How was that? The idea is to help you relax and set you up for some of the deeper practices ahead. Keep at this until you feel calm. This means practice it for weeks, if you have to, in order to get the feel of air moving through the tense or charged-up area.

Also, think about what you do to chill out. Or what do you notice that really shifts your state of being when something is troubling you with your children. Does that activity foster connection or create distance? If it leaves you numb, running away from it all, de-energized, hung over, with a scary gut reaction, then, sorry, but it isn't OMing that you are doing. We are naturally inclined to want balance within ourselves, so you are probably already creating OM Moments somehow in your life. Do you go to the gym, out with friends, laugh, eat fun food? Do you get so absorbed in the feeling of the activity that it relaxes you?

You can do practice above in many places: while standing in an elevator, sitting at a red light in your car, or rocking in your favorite chair (I have a glider rocker that has been my place to OM the biggies in my life for years).

If this is newer to you, practice this at least once a day throughout the week. You will really enjoy this once you start connecting to your body this way!

If you are really hepped up about something, like your toddlers or teens have you scattered, or you are worrying a lot about your child, return to this basic calming practice. Once you are familiar with this, it is so easy to "drop" into.

OM 102

Suspending judgment . . .

Suspended judgment is a mental state that starts to release you from the intense negative or positive emotions or thoughts you are having, that are distracting you from whatever you need to do. Suspending judgment is the beginning of moving deeper into the benefits of OM Moments. It is about neutralizing your thoughts or feelings.

Think about the situation that is troubling you — the one you identified at the beginning of this section. Start by doing exercise #12-1 from above. This time, notice thoughts that come up. Some typical examples are: "Why can't I do this?" "This is crazy!" "But it's true, I AM exhausted." "It's right for me to worry about my son." "They really are being bratty." You get the idea.

When you feel relaxed in your body, you might have new thoughts: "This is good." "More of this!"

Not allowed! Such thoughts are not neutral. They put a value on your relaxation. The idea is to just notice the feeling of relaxation.

Exercise #12.2: Judgement Be Gone!

1) Tell yourself the opposite of your thought. If you are thinking, "This will never go away," say, "This will go away."

2) If something feels big and overwhelming, say, "This is small and no big deal."

3) Really try on neutrality. To your thoughts or feelings, say, "This is neither good nor bad."

4) Get up and move. You will have to stop your focused breathing, but moving frequently distracts our mind and disperses our spiraling feelings and thoughts.

5) Remember to return to your breathing.

When thoughts arise, just let them go. Return your focus to your breathing and creating a space of neutrality. Neutrality is hard! So here is an exercise to help acquire it while you are breathing, running, sitting at a red light, etc.

Exericise #12.3: The Beautiful Neutral Zone

Become aware of your body:

1) Notice where you are tense, notice where you are relaxed

2) Resist saying to yourself that this is good or bad.

3) If judgmental thoughts arise, just let them float in and then out and hold a space for neutrality.

Suspending judgment on our experience, while key to the benefits of OM Moments, is something that takes practice. It gets you out of thinking and feeling about the very thing that is troubling you. It gets you into that alpha or theta zone so you can see what really needs to happen and act on it in a relaxed way.

Taking time to OM daily for a couple weeks will help you find possibilities and solutions that you haven't seen thus far. You will be able to move through the situation that is challenging you in an inspired way that will benefit you and your child, so keep at it. You will get it!

OM 103

Surrendering . . .

This is a great strategy for times when your efforts with your children or parenting partners aren't working. Or when you are so sure you are right, but nobody seems to give a hoot! Or when you just are not getting anywhere. But first, what does surrendering mean in this context?

> "Surrender is complete acceptance of what is, knowing it will all be okay, even witt my input".
>
> The TinyBuddha

When you surrender, you are no longer in your reasoning brain, you have invited in your intuitive brain. You are "knowing" on an elevated level; you are able to have ideas that are based on rapid processing your brain can do when it's not engaged in "this is right" or "this is wrong" thinking.

It's hard to accept the Tiny Buddha concept of "even without my input" when you are a responsible parent. You might wonder how wise such a strategy is when dealing with a two year old. But unless you're facing a safety issue that needs immediate response, surrendering can be great. You will find that you are being very responsible in doing this, though, and that what you do or don't do with your challenge will be revealed to you. It does require practice and a leap of faith!

What I like about both of the following practices is that they let you acknowledge all your feelings and thoughts about what is NOT going well. Doing that lessens the intensity of your experience, especially when your aim is to surrender to not having any input, at least temporarily, in order to have a good outcome.

Set yourself up for this by doing the previous practices, practice #12 – 1 and #12 – 2 first.

Pay attention to what comes up over the next 24 hours — what people say to you, what words you notice, what ideas come to you. Listen. If you feel bombarded by worries, fears, judgments, or thoughts, the next practice, Exercise #12 – 4, is a fabulous way to get rid of them! It's fun to do, too. It is adapted from work by Joe Vitale, a very creative problem solver. If you don't have a whiteboard, just grab a piece of paper and cross things out instead of erasing them. Cross them out so you truly can't see them anymore. If you have access to a whiteboard, it's pretty powerful, so use it! Do this with your kids, too, if they are struggling with something. Or, do it as a family if together you are all working through something like a move, a change in income, a change in who is going to work, etc.

Exercise #12.4: Peaceful Surrender

1) Get a whiteboard or piece of paper.

2) Fill it up with all the thoughts going through your head about your challenge. Fill it until there is no more space.

3) Now gradually start to erase the thoughts. Think about your challenge.

4) As new thoughts pop up, write them on the white board.

5) Now erase them.

6) Keep doing this until you have no more thoughts popping up.

7) Stare at the white board and say or think, "I ask for guidance." Sit with that.

The better you get at this, the better you will be better able to relax into challenges and work things out with your child. Conversations, ideas, actions will click into place much more easily because the situation will be clearer and you will feel calm.

Honestly, sometimes the solution you come to may seem a little unusual. Like when you hear "Do nothing" about something you were so sure you needed to do a, b or c about. Or you get, "Talk to him/her" when you were so sure you needed to just walk away/boot them out. This is when problem solving gets truly creative. It is what happens when you surrender.

In summary, there are many ways to give yourself OM Moments: running, walking, dancing, laughing, meditating, being with friends, and more. For OM Moments to be truly effective for you, you need to connect to your body, release from judgment, and surrender to the moment. Then, even if the original behavior continues, your reaction to it will be different.

One round of OMing isn't likely to be the end of your challenge. But it will help you in terms of where you are at with it RIGHT NOW. Because OM Moments get you out of a hole you are digging. But some holes are bigger than we realize. If you keep practicing and paying attention to how you move into OM Moments, you might just find you don't call your challenge a challenge anymore!

OMING IN EVERYDAY PARENTING

As a parent, learning how to find calm was similar to the challenge of listening for me. In many ways, those early years of parenting were actually the OM Moment; I was calmed by hanging out with my daughter at the lake on the way to daycare and work, I was calmed by reading her stories at bedtime, I was calmed by becoming immersed in her imagination as she unfolded an event with her stuffed animals, I was calmed by her presence. I was lucky. She was also calm by nature. Not necessarily quiet, but calm.

Going back a bit before parenting, I first heard the idea of OM through a yoga class during my twenties. Mostly, I fell asleep in that yoga class; I just couldn't maintain that alert restful state! So for years, whenever I heard the word OM, I tuned out because I knew I couldn't do that.

Fast forward to many moons later, and I started to realize I was in great need to expand my understanding of how to become calm. Those early years of parenting when just being with my daughter was an OM thing had gone. The honeymoon was over! Internally, I was always on the go, even if externally I appeared calm. And the schedule certainly wasn't calm. Then when I was laid off from my job at a Fortune 500 company and was pretty much single parenting, I truly did not know what was next. So I started into my journey toward wellness. Little did I know that I was going to truly get to know my capacity to move into OM Moments.

It didn't happen fast, but it did happen. I learned how to find the still part within me. Through somato respiratory breathing (a chiropractic technique created by Donald Epstein)[28] with spinal adjustments, reading, and listening to people more learned than me, I tuned into myself like never before. And honestly, as a parent, I needed a lot more OM Moments. Every day.

During this exploration of wellness, I discovered how easy it is to access one's OM. That incredible, expansive stillness is always, *always,* **always** in us. And when I am scattered, unsure, or overwhelmed, and easily irritated with my daughter, accessing my OM space reminds me that if I put that OM energy around my predicament, there are always, *always,* **always** better ways, even brilliant ways to go about my predicament that I just hadn't thought of. Or, I simply find restfulness even as the unsavory situation is going on. Sometimes, it turns out, I have to wait for that better way to become evident. Yet it ALWAYS works!

I also learned that I don't need to be lying on a yoga mat and free of all thoughts and feelings to get to my OM space. The glory of finding that space is that we get to work *with* our humanness, not against it. So on my chittery chattery brain days, if I go for the quiet in my body, I can start to transform that chatter. On my sluggish days, I can go for the vision of something, get some inspiration (sometimes by literally just breathing deeply — not with any particular method). I can find where there IS energy within and spread it. I can listen to music, take a next step with something, just sit in my favorite place for a while, or look at a picture of something that melts me into a loving feeling (from there I can get into the stillness easily). There are so many delightful ways to get to your OM space and strengthen your capacity to get there. One of my favorites is by looking at photos that evoke a strong, heartfelt calm feeling in me.

One morning I was particularly frazzled. So much to do, so many deadlines, so many household chores to attend to, so many things on my mind . . . you know the drill. I was fast to be irritable with my daughter before I left home and was getting more unfocused by the minute as I drove across town to a meeting.

When I had to stop for a red light, I realized I just had to stop. Stop all the chatter in my mind. For the life of me, I couldn't think how. Then I remembered a picture of a puppy that my daughter had sent me a few days earlier. I clicked on it and, slowly breathing, I looked at it. The light turned green, interrupting my attempt to "chill out," so I pulled over and stopped. I knew I needed to get into a calmer place.

Last week, this picture evoked an instant "aww" that I felt in my heart. This week, it took a bit to get the "aww." So I kept breathing as I looked at the picture and felt myself start to "soften around the edges." Then a smile came to my face. With a couple more deep breaths, I was in such a calmer place. Soon I felt the awww for this sweet puppy who found a soft, cozy, safe place to just be.

My focus returned. I had a great meeting, a productive day. And when I went home, I was a different person than I was when I'd left. I may not have gotten deeply into an alpha or theta state, but I certainly calmed down which is what was needed. OM Moments help everyday parenting moments.

Later, when my daughter came home, I offered my apology for the morning and let her know how her picture saved the day. We were able to go on and have a wonderful evening. Nothing had changed in terms of all that needed to be done, except my reaction to all of it.

Learning how to drop into OM Moments, more than anything, has moved me into my comprehension of how we are so much better than our standard learning (OM Moments can indeed take you to a different awareness, consciousness), different than our current understanding of something, and bigger than our expected role. This, more than anything, has gotten me to a point where I say, "Life is a customized experience." Because in these OM Moments, I have been allowed to see how I can seize the day in ways well beyond my initial brainy or even heartfelt understanding (or misunderstanding) of something.

Getting to my OM Moments also helped me get answers to questions like, does my daughter need medication or not, how do I help (various situations), what is really upsetting me, is this or that action creating a better life, how do I love more when I am exhausted?

Getting into the OM space is what allowed me to listen better and to better connect to the other love capacities, Voice, Visualize, and Explore. I am better able to parent with strength when I utilize OM Moments. Sometimes after getting relaxed, an answer literally lands in my email or through a comment from someone. Or sometimes whatever had my pants in a bunch ceases to affect me that way. I became confident that, even if I had to work at it a bit, by moving from my OM space, the right course of action would become clear. That is a confidence I acquired through practice and experience.

So, practice! In a loving, fun way.

CHAPTER 13

LOVE'S "V" CAPACITY – VISUALIZING AND VOICING

WHAT IS VOICING AND VISUALIZING?

> Visualizing! It's the cinema of our minds. It's going on all the time.
>
> The cinema gets better if we can slow down the mind enough to capture it, edit it, and produce it as we desire.
>
> Natasha Solovieff

You get double action in this capacity! "V" is for Visualizing and Voicing. They do go together, so worry not.

Central to the "V" capacity is the world of feelings. Yours. Seeing your truth with your mind's eye and speaking with that in mind. You do it all the time, so this is about doing it consciously, intentionally. Ask yourself what characteristics you want to be present in a situation and how you can say things to support that goal.

In general, life, including our challenges, plays out in the world of feelings. For instance, it's not just that your daughter dresses "inappropriately," or your son is "not thinking beyond the tip of his nose," or that "I'm the only one who plans things in advance," or that "I'm lost and just haven't a clue what to do next." Your *feelings* about these situations are what make them challenging. Another parent might not be bothered at all by a daughter dressing the same way as yours, or how far into the future their son thinks, or that she is the planner in the household, or that he is uncertain about what comes next. It's *your* experience of a situation that matters.

When we react to our children's behaviors, what we are voicing (verbally or nonverbally) is fueled by what we are visualizing. We might imagine the consequences of some behavior. We might imagine what people will say. Or we might flashback to our own previous experience. This visualizing and voicing becomes a feedback loop in our mind, not unlike a video that is on constant replay.

In parenting, this feedback loop starts from the beginning, at pregnancy or even before for some! We enter into parenting with ideas about what we want for our child. We even imagine what our child will turn out like. All this is based on what we've learned about being a parent from our own parents (even if we've just learned how we don't want to parent) and others around us. This view of parenting, then, is from the frame of reference of our younger selves. It is potent! And made more potent by the fact that there are layers of learning we often aren't even aware of it. It is our reactions as we move through parenting that expand our awareness.

For instance, when your six year old daughter walks out in polka dots and stripes (showing her belly, to boot), the first thing to pop up in your mind might be a negative comment your own mother said when you wore a certain outfit. You can even see her saying it! So you decide to NOT voice any concerns about daughter's attire because you don't want to be like your mother. But then you might start to feel powerless. OR, you might just blurt out the same comments your mom made! So when you part ways with your daughter that morning, you're wishing you hadn't said what you said, but you weren't able to stop yourself, and you have left behind a defensive, upset daughter. And this just keeps happening. After a while, you feel like your relationship is slipping away. You feel guilty!

Interactions like this abound as your child gets older. It could be that you value sports for boys and your son wants to do ballet. What do you picture when your son comes and tells you he wants to do ballet? And how does that affect how you respond? And how he responds? And round and round it goes.

How many times have you gone through the loop of seeing a consequence in your mind's eye (visualizing), that led to voicing something automatically, and that in turn leads to another loop of seeing (visualizing) something more worrisome, which leads to a louder voicing (within yourself or to your child)? If you are like most parents, it's been quite often.

The good news is, you've paid attention to some of this already through practicing the Listening and OM exercises!

Since feelings and mental images go together, let's back up a bit and discuss the development of feelings. There are books to help children recognize different feelings, books with faces for happy, sad, angry, hungry, grumpy, sleepy, loving, frustrated, and so on. This is important for children to learn because it helps them get organized around their feelings. Such books imprint on their brains a word describing something they experience and a visual of that experience. Yet we seem to forget about this for ourselves! When in life did you stop being with *the feeling* and its image, its sense within you? Listening and giving yourself OM Moments will help reconnect you.

As a baby, you cry. Your caretaker says, "Oh, that wet diaper makes you so unhappy!" You develop different cries for unhappy, wet diaper, impatient hunger, meltdown sleepy. You develop different facial expressions to let others know you are happy or frustrated, etc. And that continues to toddlerhood.

Toddlerhood, however, is a time when expression of feelings can start to get muted. The feelings don't, but the expression of them does. Toddlers are learning about so many things. And it's fun as a parent to watch all that learning. Yet what happens is we start to focus on the words for "doing" things and not so much on words for "being," i.e. feelings. And that can have long-lasting consequences. Say your child is learning to write but feels uncertain and no one helps her identify that feeling. She might develop a mental image of writing and that sense of unease around it. Then every time she goes to write, bam, there is the unease.

As we grow up, depending on the awareness in those around you, feelings take a back seat to the rest of our vocabulary. And as we progress in years, thinking is more valued than feeling. Feelings are so unruly! Perhaps we are getting better with this, but it takes a lot of intentionality to not accept our culture's higher value on thinking.

Meanwhile, it is vital to work with your toddlers on up to develop language around feelings. Not just the biggies of happy, sad, angry. But also of the more nuanced ones: silly, affectionate, frustrated, confused, uncertain, eager. Your child will even start to point yours out to you! Which is great, because your parenting role is going to take you into all kinds of feelings! And when you can't say what you are feeling, you are in a diminished problem-solving mode, you have diminished empowerment, and things get worse, not better. You'll just spin around in all the images marching across your brain.

The need to move into our feeling realms as a parent is really a blessing! Parenting gives us the great opportunity to get in touch with and expand ourselves because we have to learn to pay attention to ourselves if we are going to have enjoyable relationships with our children. And by doing this, frankly, we become better at all of life. Wow, now that is a deal!

For both Visualizing and Voicing, it is essential to have a feeling vocabulary, to know how you feel and how to talk about it. This is easier for some, harder for others, depending on their temperament and style of communication (take the assessment offered for free here; older children might want to take it, too).[29]

Feelings and mental images go together, whether you express your feelings or not. What does Visualizing have to do with Voicing? The mind does not operate using words, but pictures.[30]

Aside from literally seeing things, we also see mental images while talking and listening. This is the cinema of our hearing unfolding in our minds. We hear and talk in pictures, to which we react. The trick is to slow the images down so you know what you are picturing, and therefore what you are reacting to!

For instance, if someone says to you, "I saw this great car," right away you see in your mind's eye what you think is a great car. But your buddy has seen a different kind of car. You might both appreciate great cars, but until you see your idea of a great car, you are not as excited as your buddy.

If someone says, "You dummy," what picture pops into your head? What is your feeling about it? Ask a few other people what pops into their head. It will vary, no doubt. By the time you are parenting (even if you are a teen parent), you have history with your feelings and what you see in your mind's eye around them. You have reflexive reactions to many life events based on your history with your feelings. Some are embedded in your brain's reticular activating system, or RAS (refer back to Chapter 11, under Listening 103). So much of how you react to your child has a basis in your history with certain feelings, the sensory and visual memory of them. Consciously or unconsciously, they have become the basis of your value and belief system (my kid will go to college, my kid will not suffer, my kid will be respectful, my kid will be crazy, saying "no" is mean).

I bring up the RAS again to say that when, as a parent, you are not getting anywhere with some issue, it's time to consider that your response to the issue is embedded deeper in your brain, stashed away from earlier in life. Remember, it's just the brain's way of being efficient! So when we hear an idea, see an action, sense or experience a feeling, we react from the foundation of experience we've stashed in our RAS. You know, that knee-jerk reaction.

Sometimes that serves us well throughout life. Many times, it ceases to. In parenting, we know it's no longer serving us when communication (Voicing) with our children isn't going well. We can understand *our part* in how things have gone wrong if we can notice this, slow down so we can see the images in our mind's eye, and know our associated feelings. This gives us what we need to know in order to change or alter our communication. Guaranteed!

WHAT CAN I DO?
STOP. GET INTENTIONAL. VISUALIZE. VOICE.

Voicing and Visualizing are so connected. One couple I worked with told me they had been arguing. Not only was it unpleasant for them, but they were rightfully concerned about their three week old daughter picking up on the tension (babies are mood sponges). However, once a fight began, there seemed to be no stopping it, especially for the Mom. They kept digging a bigger hole in their relationship. They eventually agreed that if one of them held up a hand, both would stop and walk away. They wouldn't approach the topic again until they were calm enough or I was visiting them. They did it for a week and had a better week. But I wanted the mom in particular to discover what was driving her unease. At our next visit I asked her to tell me where the unease was showing up in her body (Listening), where there was calm in her body (Listening and OMing), what she saw in her mind's eye (Visualizing), and how she was experiencing what she saw, and how she was expressing that (Voicing).

It took her three hours, but she got it out. She saw how she was reacting to terribly unpleasant events in her past. She was visualizing a LOT; it wasn't just one or two situations but a whole web of events. She got to see her past, voice it, and then see and voice how the current situation was parallel. She was feeling awful about how she was responding, because she wants something very different for her daughter than had occurred in her own life.

The next visit we discussed re-visualizing her response to the current situation and how to voice it differently. Again, it involved the Listening and OMing steps because this was pretty complex for her (exercises #14-2 and #14-3). But she did it! And what a difference it has made for her. For them. Because she could imagine (see/visualize) something different, she could then come up with different words and a different attitude.

WHAT DO YOU LOSE IF YOU DON'T DEVELOP YOUR "V" CAPACITY?

If you don't develop a feelings vocabulary and get good at seeing the pictures that go marching across your brain when you are reacting to your toddler hitting someone, or your tween wanting to be on social media all the time, or your teen getting a D in a course you thought essential to their future, you will:

- ✓ Escalate the situation beyond where it needs to be. I see it all the time. I've done it! Backtracking can be done, thank goodness, but in the meantime, life can go off on some unnecessary pathways!
- ✓ Lose the joy in your relationships.
- ✓ Create confusion.
- ✓ Become fatigued.
- ✓ Over- or underreact.
- ✓ Pass along life patterns you really didn't want to.
- ✓ Disempower yourself, which is not what you want as a parent.

The good news is, using the pictures in your head helps figure this all out. Intentional Visualizing is a powerful way to manage challenges!

WHAT DO YOU GAIN BY DEVELOPING THE "V" CAPACITY?

So what happens when you start using your V capacity intentionally?

- ✓ Communication actually gets easier (notice I didn't say easy).
- ✓ Communication takes less energy.
- ✓ The understanding that comes out of the conflict leads to clearer solutions.
- ✓ You can reconnect to your love for your child when you get disconnected.

When you slow down your responses and start Visualizing and Voicing, you'll start noticing that some responses aren't helping, like ranting at a sullen teen or clumsy toddler, or that some things are easier to deal with than others, like you might enjoy helping with homework, but get impatient helping a child figure out a relationship issue. It's valuable to notice these things because you can acknowledge them in family relationships and team up with others to use their communication strengths where needed. Or, you can work to get better at something you never imagined getting better at!

Paying attention to your "V" capacity sometimes means simply noticing your feelings in addition to listening to your kid's feelings (*Listening 101 and 102*) and then renegotiating a solution.

Sometimes paying attention to your V capacity is also supported by the exercises in OM Moments. If you are getting stuck in the same response, the same conflict, the same result with your child, you are meeting something within your RAS that needs to be intentionally re-directed.

Let me give you an example: a mother whose toddler son won't listen when she sets limits. It turns out she didn't have a lot of limits when she was growing up. There was good and bad to that: She liked the freedom, but also felt she had too much responsibility at times. Plus, she saw that her parents weren't setting limits because they were going through things that prevented them from caring for her. As a Mom herself, she was really ambivalent about setting limits with her son. Her feelings related to her early years were triggered by this requirement of parenting (setting limits). And she was having a lot of anxiety attacks. Her toddler picked up on her ambivalence and anxiousness. Sometimes he would manipulate by acting cute. And sometimes he would get really upset. Since she didn't pay attention to her underlying feelings about setting limits, limit-setting became more and more problematic.

On the other hand, the father could see his ambivalence in the same scenario and realized that he associated setting limits with anger and hostility. He was able to instantly release from that and imagine (Visualize) a different approach and a different outcome. He could say the same thing he said before, "Stop that!," but it worked because the energy, the feeling around it, was so different (exercise #14-3)! You can't fake that kind of result; you have to give life the kind of attention he did.

You can change your challenge, too! Do your Listening and OM Moments activities on your challenge. Sometimes the release from "the old" isn't instantaneous because there are layers of "old." You get one part, then you get the next.

A note of caution: If this is bringing up something that was truly traumatic for you, find a safe, good listener and support yourself as you move through it. There is no need for you to suffer through on your own, yet again.

It is amazing that loving a young one can bring you right back to your own self. In the end, it is a gift because it is liberating. And it will definitely take you to a better place for and with your child.

Below you will find some practices you can try, whether your challenge is huge or a minor annoyance. When doing these practices, two things are important:

1. Feelings
2. There is an underlying assumption that you are approaching these practices desiring that your parent-child communication come out of love

VISUALIZING AND VOICING 101

Holding it . . .

The key to visualization is not the specifics of what's being said or the outcome. It is the feeling of a conversation, an outcome, an action. By focusing on the feeling, you leave the door of life open to more than one way of achieving the specific. So even if in the Visualization you are seeing specifics, it's the feeling about them that is important.

Hold your parenting challenge in your mind's eye.

Exercise #13.1 Seeing the Details

1) Think about the challenge you identified.

2) What are you picturing as you think about that challenge?

3) You might need to slow it down (our mind movies can occur in a nanosecond) – write it out or draw it.

4) What are the feelings being expressed?

5) What are YOUR feelings as you imagine the scenario?

VISUALIZING AND VOICING 102

Hanging out with it . . .

This is about being with your challenge. The idea is to just hang out with it in your own headspace, trying on different scenarios for unfolding it. It's like the silent practice that athletes and musicians use.

Exercise #13.2 Voicing and Visualizing from the Child Within

1) Imagine your child is with you, listening, not responding.

2) Just hold this for a while, noticing your feelings and thoughts and actions.

3) Now visualize your child responding and you responding back. Your task here is to maintain the feeling environment in the love zone.

4) Try on different scenarios: communicating in person, in writing, by phone ...

5) What's it like to switch to what you want to be like? If it's hard, return to the Listening and OM Moments exercises.

6) Keep at it over the day/week/month – however long it takes.

If one of the things you are struggling with is how to say something in a way that your child will hear, then take a look at Gary D. Chapman's book *The Five Love Languages of Children*.[31] It will help you realize that how we hear love, know we are loved, is different for different people! Or, you can just relax with some OM Moments and it will come to you. You want to get into that alpha state that improves finding solutions and making better decisions.[32]

Sometimes we get stuck and don't say what needs to be said. The following practices will help you get ready to say what once was uncomfortable to say. They activate the energy and neuro pathways around your voice box, and raise your awareness of Voicing.

Exercise #13 .3 Voice Your Gems

1) Ask yourself "What about this is important to me?" and write out your answer.

2) Then ask "What about THAT is important to you?"

3) Keep going until you've gotten to the core. You'll know you're there because a sense of peace will prevail.

AND

Exercise #13.4 Awakening Your Voice

1) Focus your breathing so it comes from the bottom of your spine up to your neck.

2) Feel your breath moving in the front of your neck as you inhale and exhale.

3) Breathe a few times or until you can feel the air moving through the front of your neck.

4) Now breathe up from your spine and have the air come to the back of the neck.

5) Breathe a few times with air going up the back of your neck.

> 6) Now breathe the air up from the bottom of your spine and imagine the breath going from the front of your neck, straight through to the back of your neck.

This is a simple, well, maybe not so simple, breathing exercise that you can do to support yourself in Voicing what you have to say in a loving way. Loving doesn't mean being nicey nicey, so get over that idea! It does mean *how* you say something is important. More on that in the "V" Capacity in Everyday Parenting section below.

Again, if you are getting stuck, go back to Listening and OMing. You know what they say, practice makes perfect. And you don't even need perfection. You just need progress.

VISUALIZING AND VOICING 103

Changing the energy of the feelings . . .

This is another way of saying change the feeling of the feelings! It's great for when you and your child are stuck in a pattern of reacting to each other's reaction. The situation is getting nowhere fast! You probably can't imagine being anything except more frustrated. This exercise is for you. It's not about the content of your thought, it's about the feeling of your thought. Therein lies the challenge of this; it is HARD to not just keep thinking the thought, to separate out the feeling you have about the thoughts.

Exercise #13.5 Envisioning Your Child

---

1) List some of the things you are really grateful for about your child.

2) Close your eyes, if that helps, and feel those things.

3) Drop into the feeling of gratefulness.

4) In that state, envision the feeling (feel the feeling) of what you want in yourself and your child.

5) State, "I let this go for the highest good of all."

6) Breathe that wonderfulness off in a vision of bubbles, balloons, a babbling brook — whatever works for you.

Sometimes it is hard to hear. So just keep repeating steps 4, 5, and 6. If you start getting agitated again, go back, feel it, and cross it out. And continue on with the question. Hint: It usually has nothing to do with the situation! Another hint: What do you notice about your child's feeling/energy and yours while you are doing steps 4 and 5?

After you have done this, you will be able to talk with your child about this challenge from the perspective of knowing what they want, underneath all their agitation! Give them what they really want from you - love, respect, or freedom - but let them know that you'll still love them and offer help. You can set a limit, state what you can't accept, negotiate, or whatever you need to do, AND give them what they want.

If your child wants both freedom and the knowledge that you still love them, it might sound like this: "I love your spiritedness. I'm sure many see it. And I know you want more freedom. I trust you with that in (list the ways). Your partying with alcohol isn't an option, though. How can that wonderful spirit of yours party without alcohol?" You get to discuss the ins and outs of drinking from their perspective, ask questions, hear their point of view, set limits, and love their desire to be more independent again and again. Loving that desire will keep bringing you back to a non-agitated response. Of course, you have to be prepared to follow up with your consequence, and, for the fact that you might have to repeat this kind of conversation. Repetition is normal. Your job is to keep calm, because otherwise your child is reacting to your energy, not to what you are saying.

Be prepared that your Voicing and Visualizing might not magically produce the results you want! The magic is that you will find yourself staying calmer and filling your child's need. You can do your part, even have fun with it, but the other variable is, of course, your young individual.

VISUALIZING AND VOICING 104

More changing the energy of the feelings . . .

The power of our thoughts is enormous. You know that statement, "If you think you can, it's true; if you think you can't, it's true"? Building your capacity to Voice and Visualize from a place of love, since that is what we want with our children, will take you to heights you didn't know you had!

Here is a visualization that will remind you of your feeling of love for your child; it will get you back into that feeling. This sounds like a strange thing to say because it's your kid — of course, you love them! In the real world, there will be times when something about your child tries you to your core. As one parent said to me about her very normal, actively exploring toddler, "I love my son to bits, but sometimes he frustrates me to my soul!"

When you are at that point, or just tired and everything about your child's wants is annoying the heck out of you, do this. You can do it as you are waiting for them somewhere, or even as you are loading the dishwasher.

It's great to do as you lie down to go to sleep. Because if you are ticked off at a pattern in your relationship with your child, you think about it as you are doing these things, right? But what you want (once you've accepted you are getting nowhere) is to get into a feeling state of love, because that will have a more positive effect on you and your child. Plus, you want to lay a pathway into your connection to whatever you call your highest source that brings you what you need in order for your love to prevail. How do you get back into your parenting Love Zone, that best parenting dance?

Feel gratitude. Don't just say you're thankful, feel it.

Exercise #13. 6: Feeling the Gratefulness

1) Close your eyes and breathe, noticing your body.

2) Breathe until the agitation is gone from your body. Put on some soothing music in the background if you are having difficulty — it will distract your mind.

3) Now imagine your child's behavior in front of you.

4) Feel the feeling of it, the energy.

5) Cross it out. Use your hands and put a big "X" over it. Keep doing the "X" until the energy of it has broken up.

6) Now envision your child in front of you in a calm state. "Ask" him or her, "What do you want from me?"

One thing we keep getting reminded of in life is that the "how" and "when" of things working out are not up to us. We have to get out of the way of being our opinionated parenting selves first. Not that you aren't right, but the energy of being opinionated does not work with children over the long haul. As Coretta Scott King said, "It doesn't matter how strong your opinions are. If you don't use your power for positive change, you are, indeed, part of the problem."[33] Before we can get into the energy for positive change, we have to get out of our own way sometimes.

The Visualizing and Voicing growth curve is a lively one. Go back and look at the Listening and OM Moments practices. Do whichever one pops out at you if you find you get stuck or it's making you even more frustrated. It might also be a good time to just put it aside for a bit. Take a walk, talk to a friend, watch a movie, close your bedroom door and read a book once you know your children are safe. Do something that makes you and your children laugh together. Return to Visualizing and Voicing growth later!

VISUALIZING AND VOICING IN EVERYDAY PARENTING

In my world, visualizing was something one did with regards to work goals. Then as I learned more about it, I realized I had begun doing it as a child when I did "silent practice" to help learn music pieces or when I practiced for typing class by envisioning the keyboard in my head as I wandered around my 9th grade hallways. I also used it when I was losing weight, imagining pushing a plate away before finishing the food and feeling really satisfied with the conversation at the table. Those are all great visualizations!

It wasn't until this past decade that I starting appreciating how much visual mental activity we have going on all the time. When I started paying attention to my mental envisioning, I realized how it added potency to whatever I was feeling in parenting.

I also realized that I frequently asked clients in my home nursing work, "What do you see happening?" "What does that look like with regards to parenting?" And the answers I got clued me in to how much I, as a parent, am visualizing outcomes, conversations, events. And what I envision makes a huge difference in what I react to, what I say, and perhaps most important *how* I say it.

Sometimes, looking back on a situation that upset me at the time, it just seems so funny! That's the value of hindsight. At the time, though, these situations always have such urgency. I recall my reaction to getting out the door in the morning. My daughter was a slug. She had no sense of time, even as late as sixth grade! Yet, she had been getting herself ready since she was three years old. Her pace and in-the-momentness was beautiful in a world with no schedules, but that wasn't my world. So every morning was a setup for anger. It took me a year or so (yes, I know, not very good problem solving) to settle myself down and take a look at what I was thinking and expecting. I imagined people standing at my work door, waiting for me with their urgent questions and then their complaints to higher ups if I wasn't there on time. And then I saw myself with my checkbook, trying to pay the bills without this job. So I took a deep breath and decided to back up to how I wanted mornings to go.

I love mornings! And part of my dilemma was that I was drawn to my daughter's way. In the end, once I saw where my tension was coming from, it was so easy to fix. I had *to see the morning*[34] of my desire. This simple problem had been loaded for me. I unloaded it by shifting what I was seeing in my mind's eye, my mind movie. My daughter and I talked about what I'd like mornings to be like. She was in agreement and of course didn't want anger coming at her. Honestly, at five years old she couldn't change. So I needed to. I moved the clocks forward twenty minutes! We started having lovely and loving mornings. And that continued, for the most part, forever. Now, she is aware of the clock on her own.

That's a simple example. Imagine how this could work on more complex issues, like worrying that your son or daughter is using drugs, will not get into college because they are getting Cs or worse, might be bullied for being different, is feeling lonely and depressed, is such a hot shot or vamp that an unplanned pregnancy is possible, is spoiled and wants the latest and greatest technology . . . recognize any of these?

These are things that of course parents would be upset about! How you talk about an issue will open or close your relationship with your child, will lead to meaningful dialogue and solutions or lock down all communication. There will also be times when what you are visualizing, imagining, is right on! Then it is good to move into OM Moments for yourself so you can then say what needs to be said in a loving way. A parent I know had to address her teen's obsessive pot smoking and associated behaviors. She was able to say, "While you are living here, pot smoking isn't an option. Nor is stealing money for your habit. Nor is lying about it all. You are going to rehab. I love you. This isn't a behavior we expect or accept of you." She could stand firm but calm in the resistance that came her way. She could remember her love for her child. Visualizing is not about avoiding reality. It is about picturing yourself dealing with reality in a loving way. Visualizing an outcome for another doesn't work very well. Visualizing how you will manage a situation does. That is part of what makes it hard for parents, because parenting is so other (child) oriented. The L.O.V.E. capacities are all about the parent side of the relationship.

In this circle of parenting capacities, you get better at what you Visualize and Voice as you get better at Listening to yourself. This is not the kind of thing that once you're good at it you never have another problem. It is the kind of thing you get good at, so you get quicker at noticing yourself and others in situations and you go deeper within for life-enhancing, loving solutions.

CHAPTER 14

THE "E" CAPACITY: EXPLORING

WHAT IS EXPLORING?

Exploring means that you are going beyond your usual, the familiar. We experience this when we slowly walk with the 18-month-old who sees ants and is enthralled. A family vacation to a national park or new city is certainly an exploration. But I am talking more about the journey into new topics, ways of learning, technology, health issues, and relationships. Parents go beyond their usual all the time; children take moms and dads outside the box of what they are used to. It could be that you are a father who wants a son who plays football and gets one who loves ballet. Or perhaps your child has ADD/ADHD, presenting challenges that you never expected. Perhaps you have a superstar child and you're a private, quiet person. Or perhaps you have to go outside your box because technology is blindsiding you, yet you really click with your child.

Even pre-Google, children took their parents outside of their usual: Previous generations of parents didn't know how to respond to girls wearing jeans, boys growing their hair long, girls going to college, couples living together without getting married! Changing social norms have long challenged parents.

Becoming a parent now means you have a lot of information coming your way. And everyone has an opinion; your decisions become political. Claire Dederer describes it well when she says, "It starts with pregnancy: Do you hit the KFC or do you eat bulgur? It moves on to birth: Do you believe in natural child-birth or are you flipping open your cell phone right this minute to schedule a C-Section? Home birth or hospital? Circumcise or not? Breast-feed or bottle-feed? Continue working or stay home? Let the baby 'cry it out' or sleep with you in your bed? Stroller or sling?" She goes on to say, "Regular life seldom presents us with dichotomies, especially dichotomies that are so fraught with philosophical underpinnings. These choices could be overwhelming."[35]

As listed in Chapter 1, the number of things that have multiple points of view is long now! And there is a ton of data. As a parent, when you really aren't sure about something that's affecting your child and you want to parent well, you become an explorer.

> Compared to all that is out there, we are all limited in our knowledge and experience.
>
> Natasha Solovieff

Where do you start, and how do you keep going without become dizzy? Whether starting with a gut feeling or just with a question, to explore anything beyond our usual, we have to be willing and open to changing our perspective, expectations, and/or attitude. We need curiosity. It helps to remember that compared to all that is out there, we are all limited in our knowledge and experience.

To explore we have to be able to manage those OMG! moments when we feel overwhelmed. Like when you discover your 16-year-old is posting nude photos on social media and you don't know what to do but yell. What should I do, how will this affect her future, why in the world would she do this, how will it affect her at school? Suddenly, we are thrust into exploring something we never even imagined.

> "Gut feelings are the tools for an uncertain world – data creates only an illusion of certainty."
>
> Gerd Gigerenzer

Once we start answering our questions or exploring based on our gut reaction, we need to be learn what experts and other parents say about how to handle such a situation, why it happens, what are the best home practices for technology access, child development, etc.

What do you do when you have the equivalent of a master's degree in a topic after Googling information your challenge? What do you do with how the information affects you? How do you know what's best for your child? Which line of thought do you follow?

Some of the practices below will help you with all of this. Also, some people just follow experts they like, the ones who pull together info in a way they understand. When it gets complicated, and all of your reading on a topic is not helping, go back to listening to yourself and your child (your "L" capacity), taking some time to calm yourself (your "O" capacity) so you can hear beyond the information and check things out with your vision (the "V" capacity). It helps to have compassion for yourself; you are not alone! We all strive to make things certain when it comes to our children. In fact, all of life is uncertain.

WHAT DO YOU LOSE WHEN YOU DON'T EXPLORE?

When we don't explore we:

- ✓ leave ourselves with fewer options,
- ✓ are dependent on our own limited experience, or on that of a professional or friend. It can be easy to make a situation worse, spend money unnecessarily, and hamper our child's growth and development,
- ✓ can waste our time and energy wishing for something instead of dealing directly with what's possible,
- ✓ don't give ourselves the support we need; we feel isolated and like "we are the only ones."

It does indeed take a village to raise a child. We are lucky and unlucky to be living in the age of Google.

WHAT DO YOU GAIN BY EXPLORING?

There are several things we gain by developing our capacity to explore:

- ✓ expanded options
- ✓ hope in the face of discouragement or despair
- ✓ vision beyond our current understanding or point of view
- ✓ spiritual growth as we push against our mental boundaries
- ✓ a village of support

When we allow ourselves to explore beyond our usual, we start opening up to new possibilities. Frequently when we are challenged, we experience some sort of despondency about the situation. By opening up to exploring, we get to go beyond that despondency, into options, into hope.

In his book, *The Anatomy of Hope*, Dr. Jerome Groopman writes, "I understand hope as an emotion made up of two parts: a cognitive part and an affective part. When we hope for something, we employ, to some degree, our cognition, marshalling information and data relevant to a desired future event. . . You have to generate a different vision of your condition in your mind. That picture is painted in part by assimilating information. . . Belief and expectation — the key elements of hope — can alter neurochemistry by releasing the brain's endorphins and enkephalins, mimicking the effects of morphine."[36]

The mind, body, spirit connection is alive and well in the simple act of Googling. We can acquire hope by exploring the why, what, where, when, and how of a situation that is new to us. This sounds so simple, but it isn't always so.

Take for instance the mother we considered earlier, whose son is acting up. Because she has decided her son is just like she was when she was a kid, she doesn't really explore other options for why he might have trouble when limits are set. The "why" of his trouble is a foregone conclusion to her. She closed herself off to learning more about her son and herself. She had no hope for any different outcome so continued on in frustration.

Next are the practices that can support us in more easefully strengthening our "E" Capacity.

EXPLORING 101

Acceptance . . .

To explore outside your box, you need curiosity. Embedded in curiosity is acceptance. So congratulations — you have accepted that what you are doing isn't working/ you need help/ your child needs help. You are open, willing to delve into an unknown for you.

> Acceptance is NOT saying "This is agreeable, okay." It is you getting to a point where you are neutral about it: "Oh, here it is." You aren't denying, resisting, or judging the situation. It just is. It's preparation for the best action.
>
> Natasha Solovieff

Let's first be clear, acceptance is not saying that you are fine with everything as it is. It is when you get to a point where you are neutral about what is going on; it is neither good nor bad, big nor little. You are just dealing with it because it is something with which to deal.

Acceptance comes in stages. Some situations are easy to find information about because they aren't loaded with right and wrong — like, what's the best sunscreen for my baby?

Other things you might have more feelings about, like how to deal with a wheat allergy in a family when your parenting partner denies allergies exist and says they only happen to wusses?

When you are in a situation for which you just can't access nonjudgmental acceptance, this practice might help:

Exercise 14-1 Uncluttering your Decision Making Space

1) Grab some blank pieces of paper. For your eyes only.

2) Write all the things that go through your angry or scared mind.

   a. Do not evaluate your statements!

3) Fill as many pages as you can. Write everything, no matter how small.

4) Sleep on it.

5) Get up, read through it, and then burn it. Keep doing this until you no longer have angry or fearful thoughts.

Say the challenge is that your child doesn't transition from one situation to another easily. When it's time to leave for school, all kinds of procrastinations emerge. When it's time to leave the party, suddenly there are all these people to talk with. When it's time to do homework, tiredness descends. You initially think, "My child has no respect for my schedule." You start to hate departures because they always lead to an argument. You become convinced your kid is lazy when it comes to deadlines. Notice how it can spiral downward.

After you've gotten into acceptance, a neutral zone, come up with three new ways of interpreting the situation; they must leave you in that neutral zone or it's back to the practice above! What does a positive spin achieve? For instance, with the homework, it might be that your child doesn't like the subject (we've all been there), or that he or she feels uncomfortable in the class, or finds it boring. It has nothing to do with lazy!

These activities help neutralize your emotions about the issue, take the heat out of it. They help you open your mind beyond your initial negative interpretation (in the sense that it is not moving you into constructive problem solving *with* your child). Your attitude, understanding, and expectations can keep you from discovering what's really going on with your son or daughter. And then you might not be accurately focused while Googling away for solutions. Change your attitude and understanding, and you might not have to Google anything!

If you find yourself resisting this (not getting to this practice, doubting everything you read or hear, getting really irritated while doing these activities), throughout the activity you can affirm the direction you are going by saying something like, "I am learning there are options I didn't know existed," or "I am discovering more ways to think about _____," or "I am just taking a look to see what else is out there about this." Gradually, you will find yourself in greater acceptance and exploring will lead you to a better solution for your challenge.

Sometimes it's hard to move from being aware something isn't working to acceptance. We get stuck going round and round our challenge: how this wasn't supposed to happen, this isn't fair, this wasn't what I planned, what should I have done differently, how can I keep this from getting real bad, I must be an awful parent, Under all of this is anger and fear. So keep returning to practice #15-1. You *will* land at the doorway of acceptance; you will find yourself saying, "It just is what it is."

How does all this work with significant concern such as drugs, porn, sex, lying? The same way it works for the less threatening issues. Seeking to reach a state of acceptance is not about foregoing action. It is preparation for exploring best actions without all the anger and sleepless nights. The challenge will likely continue, even when you are in a state of acceptance about it. What does happen is that you will not fall apart with these challenges. If you stay with your initial interpretation and upset reactions about your child's behavior or about what you should do, you risk harming your relationship and even yourself (stress over time is harmful). Even if you are past the "concerned" stage and something is really occurring, moving into the acceptance exercise will help you respond caringly even while being decisive.

It is easy to judge any of these truly troublesome concerns, normal to be very afraid for your child, and equally normal to want to fight, flee, or freeze. In fact, the need to practice the circle of parenting capacities is great! Things will be better if you aren't freaking out every time you turn around. While it's tempting to just let it rip, it will get you nowhere but in a deeper hole. Because you are a parent, your love and fear run right next to each other. THE place to start when having great parenting challenges is with practice #15-1 because it requires you to reach out. Not only does it take a village to raise a child, it takes a village to support a parent. Find your village. Use your village. And move into growing all of your parenting capacities.

A lot of people now explore online for parenting information and solutions. Here are some thoughts on looking at different websites and deciding which are credible. Popular opinion may be interesting, but it isn't always reliable. For instance, you might read about people getting pregnant even when "on depo" (birth control shots). What they might not say is that they were a week late for the shot, which must be administered on time (plus or minus a day or two of shot's due date). So, when exploring other input through the web, look for sites with:

- ✓ Credible authors.
- ✓ If you are looking at research, look for the "n," the number of people/sample studied. The higher the better.
- ✓ An acknowledged frame of reference. For example, a church takes one frame of reference on issues, a medical doctor another, a naturalist another. Is the site knowledgeable about variables you consider important?
- ✓ An understanding of what the priority is for you: respect, health, lifestyle, future, etc.?

Look at these sites with a recognition that there are other points of view than yours. Remember, you are an explorer and an explorer has openness! This can be challenging when parenting. Very. If your daughter announces she is a lesbian, and you are morally against homosexuality, you will be challenged. You also have another value, love. So with love in mind you can explore the issue of sexual orientation. Our kids will challenge us on deeply held perspectives sometimes. Keep in mind the Chinese proverb: "Do not confine your children to your own learning, for they were born in another time."

> Because you are a parent, your love and fear (worry, fretting) run right next to each other. For that reason, parents require a village of support.
>
> Natasha Solovieff

For example, you may have smoked pot when you were growing up. Is it okay now, given the evolution of the plant? You may have gone from high school to college to marriage and work, but is that path going to be best for your child given life span changes and options available now? You may have been disciplined with the same punishment for everything, but is that going to be best for your child when there are so many more opportunities to stumble across trouble? You may have been allowed to watch anything on TV, but is that wise now with the avalanche of programming available on TV?

Every parent has nightmares about challenges they're not sure they could deal with. If and when you do land there, it will take time, patience, compassion (from and for yourself and others), time-outs from dealing with whatever it is, and the use of every single one of these capacities. L.O.V.E. will get you to good decisions and a place of peace within.

EXPLORING 102

Digestion . . .

So now you have a lot of new data. Maybe you have found out that many people have experienced your challenge. And that there are x, y, and z ways to handle it. You've found out what your friends and family members think about your predicament. But you aren't sure how you want to change course.

Exercise #14-2: Expanding Horizons

1) Ask at least three others how they would interpret the situation.

2) Ask at least three others what they would do.

3) List at least three new interpretations of your situation, without using words like good, bad, stupid.

4) List at least three ways to approach your challenge.

5) List at least three potential results of the approaches.

Now, just sit with it. That's what Maria did. Maria was concerned her seven year old son might have ADHD. She'd seen a lot of boys with this diagnosis who were big problems, so she really didn't want that. Before she started exploring solutions, she tightly structured his homework and time with friends, videogames, and household responsibilities. None of it was working and they were getting hostile to each other. She felt like a failure and she wasn't sure what he was experiencing.

After yet another argument about him playing video games too long, she admitted to herself that her approach wasn't working. She took a deep breath and started researching diagnosis and treatment of ADHD. There were a range of treatment options! It was mind-boggling. By the time she was done, she didn't have a clue what she wanted to do.

So she sat with it. Sort of. She went back to all the capacities she had practiced. For two weeks she sat with "what to do" by picking an exercise that felt right for each day. She came to her decision to get additional testing for her son because she noticed that when she was calm, the readings on getting additional testing surfaced in her mind.

This is when you decide what is negotiable and what isn't. Your sense of your child's safety, your home's harmony, your schedule, your energy levels, are all a part of this. YOU are not left out of this decision.

For instance, nonnegotiable items might be what time you leave the house in the morning, how many extracurricular activities can be pursued, how much you'll spend on birthday presents, your stance on drugs, whether cell phones are allowed in the bedroom at night, which TV shows and video games are allowed. The list is endless. This is the time to be clear about the non-negotiables.

EXPLORING 103

Choosing action . . .

Deciding what to do, especially when more than one option looks good, can be fun but tricky. You are probably familiar with writing out a list of pros and cons. Before you get to pros and cons, I recommend writing out what your priorities are regarding values and cost.

Say the challenge is about which of the three sports that your son wants to do is best for him. At the top of your paper write out your budget; whether small teams, solo sports or popular teams are important; which team attitudes and leadership characteristics are important; and anything else important in your decision. This will help you decide while including your son in the process as you go over the list together.

It's important to remember that sometimes choosing inaction is really an action. Recall our earlier example of Maria, who gave herself a couple weeks before deciding if she wanted to change anything. That was an action! It is different from avoiding or just not getting to it.

If you want to decide, and the list of pros and cons isn't working for you, here's a less cognitive way of choosing:

Exercise #14- 3 Body Talk for Decision Making

1) Notice where in your body you hold a calm feeling about your challenge (If you don't find an area of calm, go to your Listening and OMing practices).

2) Breathe into that area. As you are breathing, focus on that area. You will start to feel "movement" in it.

3) Just be in that "movement." You are connecting to the energy of that area. Lean into that energy.

4) Hold your first decision choice in that area and notice the sensation. Now hold the other decision choices in this calm area.

5) You are looking for expansion or contraction of the movement of the energy in that calm area; tightness or softness.

This kind of quietness is dynamic decision-making, choosing a direction! But not from your mind only. Our bodies don't lie! The option that causes expansion is the best decision. This is a little hard to trust at first. Therefore, try it on low-risk decisions first. Keep in mind, there are lots of different ways of knowing! Here's another.

Exercise #14-4 Weighing It All

1) Hold out both of your hands.

2) "Put" a decision choice in each hand. Which feels heavy, which feels light? Eliminate the one that feels heavy in your hand. Keep the option that feels lighter.

3) Put another decision choice in your empty hand. Which feels heavy, which feels light? You can keep comparing choices until you have only one choice. That's your decision!

When making decisions, many parents wonder at what age children should start making their own decisions. How old is old enough? There is no magic age. By involving them in your process from an early age, you'll know when they are ready to start with small decisions. Even at a young age, they can have fun with this while learning that decisions involve more than just satisfying wants. Many times they will come up with creative ways to get what they want! It can be quite amazing.

EXPLORING 104

Letting go . . .

Letting go. The prospect sends many of us into a tizzy. But what does letting go mean? It doesn't mean "I don't care anymore," "What I do doesn't matter," or "Don't come to me about . . . anymore." It does mean that you realize the outcome to a problem is not totally up to you, that you are not in control of that outcome. There are variables you can't foresee on the problem and the solution side. Even though you are the parent! It is a myth that parents have total control of how their children turn out.

And maybe, just maybe, this is a situation where you have to be willing to let your child accept whatever natural consequences come their way; it's not your job to decide on a course of action. If they are selling alcohol to minors and are found out, if they are not handing in their homework, if they insist on staying up late when they have to get up early, if they eat food they know makes them sick, perhaps the natural consequences are their best way of learning. You do need to be clear about what is negotiable and not negotiable, however.

Assuming you have done your part as a parent, utilizing all these other L.O.V.E. tools, sometimes your children's independent streak, or learning curve and learning style, or readiness to know simply needs to be dealt with through the consequences that naturally occur as a result of their behavior. It's parallel to what you might do with the physically adept, risk-taking toddler on the playground: You stay close, without crowding, but you are there if they need you. They have to learn their limits. You might stand by (spot them), but you don't hold their hand or give them instructions.

> Letting go means recognizing that there are variables you can't foresee on the problem end and the solution end. You don't have total control of the outcome.
>
> Natasha Solovieff

If they are not handing in their homework and you've been through problem-solving with them, letting them find out on their own what happens might be the best course of action. You let them know you won't say any more about it, you won't yell at them if they flunk the course (unless passing isn't negotiable), it's theirs to decide.

What do you do in the meantime? Because you will find yourself holding your breath at times, biting your lip to refrain from saying anything, fretting and stewing about it in your own private space, this might help:

Exercise #14- 5 The Love Surround

1) Return to practice #15-1 , #14-5 and #14-6.

2) Find an image that represents lovingly letting go of any expectation/desire/outcome and look at it when you are feeling stuck or anxious about letting go. Mine is:

EXPLORING IN EVERYDAY PARENTING

I started into the wellness journey that I mentioned in the OM Moments section for several reasons. One was because of some things I was noticing with my daughter. She needed ways to calm herself. She was very spiritual — naturally connected to the self and the divine. Highly sensitive. But I didn't know this at first. All I saw was that she was hesitant with others, had mood shifts that I didn't understand, and she missed school a lot because she wasn't feeling well. These big changes started to become noticeable in third grade.

I was a pretty informed mother because of my professional work as a pediatric and public health nurse. Yet my daughter wasn't making sense to me. As I stepped into this, I started talking to others, then began reading a lot. This exploration took me into learning about highly intuitive people, food sensitivities, anxiety disorders, brain balancing, medications, levels of consciousness, allergies, and normal tween and teen development. Wow!

I bumped into so many fears while reading and talking. Sometimes the fear would come across as being judgmental about my daughter, myself, or someone's point of view. Sometimes I felt scared about how things would turn out, wishing that things could be easier. Sometimes I felt frustrated that there were so many different points of view about what caused these kinds of health issues. I would want to run away from it all to a place where things felt "normal." I took many a deep breath and said, okay, time to move beyond my fears and delve into this further. Bit by bit, things began to work out. I met incredibly helpful people, professional and personal.

My daughter and I did a lot of talking through all this exploring. Because of this, by high school she was very actively involved in decisions about what would support her. For me, by becoming willing to explore, I have gained the capacity to take that deep breath and say, "Well, let's see what this might be about," for many kinds of problems even beyond parenting.

Exploring all I've had to explore has made me courageous! It has also taught me that I am never alone; there are always others out there (many times a phenomenal number of others) who know something about what I am just starting to explore. It has opened me to the world of science beyond the medical model in which I trained. It has taught me to follow my gut — it's so right on. It's taught me to look beyond someone saying "That can't be," or "You just have to live with this." It has taught me not to listen only to experts, but also to myself. These are big gifts I've gotten from developing my capacity to explore. I move into exploring more gracefully now because I've gotten better at getting out of my own way, of recognizing when I'm judging, resisting, stuck.

Was every decision a big exploration process? No. My daughter loved TV. After a few hours of it a few days in a row I'd notice changes in her behavior: not getting enough sleep, not getting homework done, not getting outside. I'd ask her what was going on with all the TV watching. She might or might not acknowledge that it was becoming too much of a good thing; she'd remind me that it relaxes her and give whatever other reason she had that day. But she wouldn't necessarily curtail it. I'd let her know I noticed she wasn't curtailing it, and that I would. She'd say, "No Mom, I'll do it myself." Sometimes she would. Sometimes, however, it got to the point of me pulling the plug. I told her I had a secret way of knowing whether she used it or not! After a couple of days she'd be thanking me for pulling the plug. We went through this cycle several times each year for many, many years. No exploring here. All I needed to do was watch her behavior and know something different needed to happen. Meanwhile, she learned other relaxation strategies!

Most parents I know are exploring a lot even though they don't always know it. A mother I know was feeling very tense and arguing with her son a lot about his time spent on video games. She would say things like "I just don't like how I'm being with him. It doesn't pay to argue. It all goes better when it comes from love." Brilliant observation. And it did! Whenever she practiced #15-1, I'd see her calm down and, with a smile on her face, come up with her next steps. Her explorations taught her a lot about video addiction, helping a son identify what he was experiencing, getting beyond her hesitancy about voicing concerns, and great ways to guide her son in expanding his life outside of gaming. Exploring is in many ways just what parents do! The trick is to do it more easefully.

I would say a mistake we parents make is thinking we'll go through our practices once, respond to our children once, and once-and-for-all things will change. In reality, we have to re-visit our L.O.V.E. practices frequently. And respond to our children about whatever the challenge is, repeatedly. The fact is, the dance of parenting is one big Exploration, supported by Listening, OMing, and Voicing and Visualizing.

CHAPTER 15

CONFIDENCE BUILDING IN EVERYDAY PARENTING

Moving through your different steps and phases of practice during your dance of parenting can be great fun, but that's only when you have confidence in your process - something that is impossible to have 100 percent of the time! To help us build our confidence, generating affirmations is so valuable. Getting to an affirmation can be tricky when we are a parent because parenting is by nature other-focused. We are tempted to affirm something like, "Steven does well on his math test," when in fact affirmations work better when they are self –focused. While we can influence our children's outcomes, ultimately the outcome is up to them. The trick to parenting affirmations is turning our focus on ourselves.

The other trick to parenting affirmations is what to do when we don't actually feel positive? We all have pretty much learned that we use positive words when doing affirmations. We also know we all have days when we don't quite feel the power of our affirmations, right? Wouldn't it be nice if there was more than one way to "speak to" an intention, a wish? Well, there is!

Natalie Ledwell teaches this process in her Ultimate Success Management class. It is vital to empowering you with your parenting affirmations; it supports this whole dance through parenting. It's actually at once a releasing, calming, and energizing process.

Start your affirmation process with the down and dirty. List out all the things you don't like about the current situation. For instance, I used to struggle with getting my daughter out the door on time in the morning and it would always end in me being annoyed and unpleasant. I wanted to change that so that mornings could be more pleasant. I listed out everything I didn't like about the current situation:

1.   I love mornings and this ruins them
2.   I don't like having to rush
3.   I don't like the guilt I feel because I got so annoyed
4.   I don't like being late

Some of my lists are longer than that!

After doing this, list why each of these is important. My list included:

1.   I love mornings and this ruins them – *mornings are a calm and upbeat time for me, I love the light outside, the sounds of the home in getting-going mode*
2.   I don't like having to rush – *rushing gets me tense and distracted, not to mention unpleasant*
3.   I don't like the guilt I feel because I got so annoyed – *it stays with me during the day and dampens my mood, starts the school day with stress for my daughter*
4.   I don't like being late – *people count on you being there when you said you were going to be there*

Next, list what you'd like (which spills right out of what is important in the above), and say what is important about each. My list about getting my mornings back included:

1.   I want calm and upbeat mornings (see how that falls right out of WHY THIS IS IMPORTANT TO ME above?) – *fuels me, home feeling*
2.   I want to get out the door knowing I have everything with me – *more organized, not feeling like I am always scrambling*
3.   School starts without stress from home – *it's a loving start to our day*

4. Mornings create a grounded feeling for the day – *I need to be grounded for all that I do, I think and create best from groundedness*
5. I am respectful of the time needs of those who need me first thing in the work day – *this is just one of the ways I show I respect another*

From there, create five types of affirmative statements based on the WHY THIS IS IMPORTANT TO ME. My list looked like this:

1. A goal affirmation: *80 percent of my mornings (I don't ask for perfection!) are organized for readiness to leave on time*
2. A thought affirmation (what kinds of thoughts are you thinking): *I am grounded by my mornings*
3. A feeling affirmation (how life feels when what you want is occurring): *I love my mornings; they are my fuel*
4. An action affirmation: *I start the day with loving activities*
5. A "why" affirmation (affirm why this is important to you): *I have a loving, homey start to the day with my daughter*

Who'd have ever thought getting out of the door in a timely manner involved so much affirming! But doing this forced me to know more about why I was getting my pants in a bundle over not leaving on time; it was in fact connected to some important values and enjoyments. Which makes sense, as mornings have always been the favorite part of my day.

This gives you some flexibility in what you want to affirm on any given day. If you aren't in your thinking brain, you can focus on the feeling or action affirmation. If you aren't into action, you can focus on the why or feeling.

Doing an affirmation process like this gets you focused on your part in the dance of parenting partnership. As with all affirmations, you keep at it until you find the statement that works for your truth right now. It will empower you as you move through all the exercises. It will keep you strong in your dance of parenting, because you are. You are here. You are engaged. You are taking care of your part of the dance of parenting. Bravo!

APPENDIX A

TASK/ACTIVITY	Mom	Dad		
kitchen dishes (wash - put away)				
laundry (wash - fold and put away)				
take out the garbage				
budget all household needs				
track budget				
pay the bills				
tax preparation				
grocery planning/ shopping				
meal preparation				
track household supply inventory				
household supplies purchase				

pick up things around house				
clean house				
get kids to brush teeth				
bedtime ritual management				
secure the house before sleeping				
household wake-up management				
breakfast prep				
get kids dressed				
get kids out to school				
manage meetings with daycare/school				
help with homework				
plan supply purchases for school/activities				
Purchase supplies for school and activities				
sign papers needed for school/daycare				

transportation for special events				
plan summer camps				
plan clothing shopping needs				
shopping for clothing needs				
Scheduling medical appointments				
Medical appointment transportation				
read to children				
play/talk with children				
resolve conflicts between children				
research child raising topics				
plan for family times				
plan extended family times				
plan and arrange adult social time				
maintain the vehicles				
household repair management				

pet feeding				
pet walking				
schedule vet appointments				
take pets to vet appointments				

ENDNOTES

1   Ursula K. Le Guin is an American author of novels, children's books, and short stories, mainly in the genres of fantasy and science fiction. She has also written poetry and essays.

2   "Parenting Through History: A Look at Childrearing in Five Historic Societies," John Farrier, Neatorama.com

3   *The Book of Household Management,* Isabella Beeton, ebooks.adelaide.edu. au/b/beeton/isabella/household/

4   "Encyclopedia of Children and Childhood in History and Society," www.faqs. org/childhood/Me-Pa/Parenting.html

5   BreastfeedingUSA.org, Sara McCall, 2014, "Nursing in Public: What US Mothers Faced from Colonial Times Until Today" https://breastfeedingusa.org/content/article/ nursing-public-what-us-mothers-faced-colonial-times-until

6   These questions are adapted from MIT open courseware: http:// ocw.mit.edu/courses/global-studies-and-languages/21g-019-communicating-across-cultures-spring-2005/ assignments

7   "The New Dad: Right at Home," Prof. Brad Harrington, Fred Van Deusen, Iyar Mazar, Boston College, 2012, www.bc.edu/content/dam/files/centers/ cwf/pdf/The%20New%20Dad%20Right%20at%20Home%20BCCWF%20 2012.pdf

8   "Is It Cooler to Be a Stay-at-Home Dad Than a Stay-at-Home Mom?," Brian Gresko and Stephanie Feldman, Salon, www.salon.com/2015/04/18/ is_it_cooler_to_be_a_stay_at_home_dad_than_a_stay_at_home_mom/

9   "Why Aren't Moms Who Take Care of Their Kids Called Heroes, Too?", Leslie Morgan Steiner http://www.modernmom.com/dcd7baf0-3b3e-11e3-be8a-bc764e04a41e.html

10 "What is it like to be a stay-at-home dad," Michael Hennessy, Quora, 2012, http://www.quora.com/What-is-it-like-to-be-a-stay-at-home-dad

11 "All work and no play with children makes moms less happy parent", University of Minnesota, October 4, 2016, https://twin-cities.umn.edu/ news-events/all-work-and-no-play-children-make-moms-less-happy-parents

12 "The Surprising Jobs That Now Require a College Degree," Chad Brooks, Business News Daily, Sept. 9, 2014, www.businessnewsdaily.com/7103-no-degree-no-job.html

13   Changing Trends In Childhood Disabilities, Amy J Houtrow, Kandyce Larson,Lynn Olson, Paul Newacheck, Neal Halfon Pediatrics.aapublications. org/content/early/2014/08/12/peds.2014-0594

14   "Childhood Mental Disabilities on the Rise," CNN, Aug. 18, 2014 thechart. blogs.cnn.com/2014/08/18/childhood-mental-health-disabilities-on-the-rise/

15   Parenting Class http://www.omgparenting.com/ the-secret-of-your-parenting-vows/parenting-love-zone-101/

16   "The American Family Today," Pew Research Center, Dec. 17, 2015, www. pewsocialtrends.org/2015/12/17/1-the-american-family-today/

17   "Study Finds Having Kids Do Chores Is a Good Thing," Kimberly Dishongh, Associated Press, July 12, 2015, www.washingtontimes.com/news/2015/ jul/12/study-finds-having-kids-do-chores-is-a-good-thing

18   "Fathers, You Can't Afford a Stay-at-Home Mom," Steven Nelms, We Are Glory blog, March 20, 2015, http://www.weareglory.com/blog/ fathers-you-cant-afford-a-stay-at-home-mom

19   *Daring Greatly: How the Courage to Be Vulnerable Transforms the Way We Live, Love, Parent, and Lead, Brené Brown*, Avery hardcover, 2012

20   "The Parenting Paradox," Belinda Luscombe, pg 42, "The Science of Happiness," a Time Special Edition, June 10, 2016

21   *Evolve your Brain*, Dr. Joe Dispenza's, Health Communications Inc., 2007

22   "Affirmations: The Science Behind Why They Work," Komarraiju Benkata Vinay, ezinearticles.com, May 1, 2009, http://ezinearticles. com/?Affirmations---The-Science-Behind-Why-They-Work&id=2294362

23   https://en.wikipedia.org/wiki/Stress - a great visual of what stress does

24   "Too Much Information: How a Data Deluge Leaves Us Struggling to Make Up Our Minds," Rikke Duus and Mike Cooray, The Conversation, July 15, 2015, http://theconversation.com/too-much-information-how-a-data-deluge-leaves-us-struggling-to-make-up-our-minds-44674

25   "Harvard neuroscientist: Meditation not only reduces stress, here's how it changes your brain." Brigid Schulte, Washington Post, May 26, 2015

26   "Looking up: Mindfulness increases positive judgments and reduces negativity bias," Laura G. Kiken and Natalie J. Shook, Social Psychological and Personality Science, July 2011, http://spp.sagepub.com/content/2/4/425

27   "The Meditative Mind: A Comprehesive Meta Analysis of MRI Studies", Maddelena Boccia, Laura Piccardi, Paola Guariglia, BioMed Research International, Junne 4, 2015 https://www.ncbi.nlm.nih.gov/pmc/articles/ PMC4471247/

28   *The Twelve Stages of Healing*, Donald Epstein, Amber-Allen Publishing, 1994

29   Communication style assessment http://www.queendom.com/tests/ access_page/index.htm?idRegTest=2288

30   BrainConnection.com, 2013, How We Remember and Why We Forget. http:// brainconnection.brainhq.com/2013/03/12/how-we-remember-and-why-we-forget/Someone with credentials who says this

31   *The Five Love Languages of Children*, Gary D. Chapman, Moody Publishers, 2012

[32] "Debiasing the Mind Through Meditation: Mindfulness and the Sunk-Cost Bias." Andrew C. Hafenbrack, Zoe Kinias, Sigal G. Barsade, Psychological Science, Dec. 6, 2013; http://pss.sagepub.com/content/ea rly/2013/12/06/0956797613503853

[33] Coretta Scott King (1927 - 2006), American author, activist, and civil rights leader

[34] Author's visualization video of what mornings are like with her daughter https://vimeo.com/89556066

[35] *Poser; My life in twenty-three yoga poses*, Claire Dederer, Picador paperback, 2011, pages 102 &103

[36] "Too Much Information: How a Data Deluge Leaves Us Struggling to Make Up Our Minds," Rikke Duus and Mike Cooray, The Conversation, July 15, 2015, http://theconversation.com/too-much-information-how-a-data-deluge-leaves-us-struggling-to-make-up-our-minds-44674

[37] *Optimism: The Biology of Hope*, Lionel Tiger, Kodansha Amer, 1995

Made in the USA
Middletown, DE
22 May 2017